Pleasure Gardens

by Phillip Watson

Design and layout by Linda Bernard of RyeType, Inc., Design and Typography.

First Edition
Printed in the United States.

Phillip's Tips

Introducing children to gardening is a fine endeavor if done properly. Notice that I didn't mention raking leaves, pulling weeds, or mowing grass. Make a spot where flowers can be planted, tended, and picked. That other and less fun part of gardening can come later. As a child, I had a small garden of my own, and I spent hours arranging my plants and admiring their various qualities. My parents could usually find me there, much the same way they could find my brother behind the barn smoking cigarettes. Good habits and good hobbies can be life-long pleasures. And that's a nice legacy.

Dedication...

To Alease,

my dearest friend on God's green Earth.

Table of Contents

Phillip's Tips

First things first. When planning a garden, consider its boundaries as part of the initial effort. Privacy issues can be resolved with property-line fences or screening plants. For close neighbors who are also close friends, remember that plantings are friendlier than fences. The double-edged sword, the rose hedge, is beautiful from both sides, AND its thorns will repel invading children!

W elcome to my *Pleasure Gardens*!

At times I got carried away when preparing this book and, like my elaborate parterre designs, I had to streamline, amend, and (in some cases) censor what flowed from my pen.

"Pleasure gardens" are typically described as public gardens, which include a variety of spectacles as well as activities. My interpretation of pleasure gardens is purely selfish with no regard for the masses and certainly no merry-go-rounds to distract from my parterre designs. When company comes, as it will, I enjoy providing a beautiful setting full of interesting details – all of which begin and end with the garden itself. When company departs, as it hopefully will, the gardens are once again mine, and they do, indeed, pleasure me.

Within *Pleasure Gardens* I have tried to present solutions and inspirations as equal partners in garden design. Just as whimsy and utility dance together in most successful garden schemes, the science of horticulture and the art of design play crucial and interactive roles.

Details abound throughout *Pleasure Gardens* to illustrate a point: many gardens are beautiful at a glance, but few improve upon close inspection. Architectural details such as birdhouses, arbors, and pavilions are obvious focal points, but smaller and still worthy, points of interest include unique containers, rarely seen plants, and subtle garden lighting.

Stories of personal *and* garden growth dot the landscape in *Pleasure Gardens*.
This book is a journey, and I have attempted to make its garden path an interesting one with rest stops along the way for reflections, digestions, or simply to laugh out loud. I come from a long line of strong personalities who planted their tongues firmly in their cheeks, led interesting lives and often made interesting choices. Such as the naming of their children…

I was born in Lexington, Mississippi, as were my father and grandfather – both of whom were named Henri Phillips Watson. I became the third in that illustrious blood line. With "Henri" as a given name, I was bound to design French-inspired parterres as a tip of the hat to my heritage.

Not so fast, dear readers. It seems that my great grandfather and his wife were expecting a girl when my grandfather was born. Having already promised to name the baby after the delivery doctor's wife, the child was cleverly named Henri, which is short for Henrietta! Only in Mississippi, folks, only in Mississippi…

I hope you enjoy *Pleasure Gardens*.

Phillip

Inspiration

The early morning sun streamed through the sidelights of the entry hall. The glass was beveled, and the floor was bathed in fragmented rainbows. As the sun rose higher, the rainbows began to stretch across the floor, and I was soon a part of them.

Rosemary Verey once told me that I would never be a very good garden designer until I'd given up everything else. Rosemary was my mentor and tormentor, all wrapped into one, and of course, the idea of a seemingly monastic life dismayed me – bon vivant and ne'er-do-well that I was. There were lots of other endeavors that I enjoyed. It took a while, but I learned to differentiate between legitimate choices and ridiculous distractions. Blurred lines didn't work for pattern gardens, and they wouldn't work within my career, either. The depth of Rosemary's words stayed with me, and the delicious truth slowly revealed itself.

In 1986, I met renowned English garden designer, Rosemary Verey, at a workshop I was attending in the South of France where she was a featured guest lecturer during my month-long stay at Château de la Napoule. I desperately needed a mentor, and my tender trap was set long before Rosemary arrived. Another esteemed English garden designer, John Brookes, was present to conduct the class on garden design and drafting techniques. However, John was a better student than I was. Each morning at 6:30 a.m., he attended my class – high-energy aerobics – and never missed a beat or session. Soon, though, I would abandon his drafting class altogether in my plot to woo Rosemary and make her mine! Up until that point, I had worked hard in all of my courses and had a perfect attendance record. That perfect record was about to crumble.

Rosemary would be at the school for only a week, so I had no time to waste. I had decided that, unknown to her, she would be the mentor who would finally get me on track. I admired her designs, her work ethic, and especially her lifestyle. Rosemary's private gardens in The Cotswolds of England were well known, as were her A-list clients. I had one week to court her, and there simply was no time for anyone else – not even our Mister Brookes!

Rosemary, of course, had no idea of my intentions. I guess she never saw the film, "All About Eve"! All kidding aside, I simply adored her and wanted her to notice me. Each day she and I began going to the beach during John Brooke's drafting class where we floated for

hours in the buoyant salt waters of the Mediterranean. My friendship with Rosemary blossomed even as my grades withered. Already, though, the big picture was coming into focus.

Shortly after my stay in France, Rosemary invited me to her home, Barnsley House in the Cotswolds of England. At last I could personally view the gardens I had only seen in books. Many more trips to Barnsley would follow including a Christmas visit when I first noticed how beautiful frost looked on perfectly clipped plants.

Rosemary frequently lectured in the United States, and soon I began helping her set up for her talks and book signings. I was fortunate enough to be able to give some "duet" lectures with her where English and American gardens were compared. Forget about the A-list; Rosemary and I were both A-types and often had battles at the microphone, which delighted our audiences, and even made us smile.

Over the years, Rosemary Verey introduced me to countless experts in the gardening field. Some were photographers, others were journalists. And all were important. Rosemary told me that if a garden couldn't be properly photographed, then it would never be published. And if it were never published, its designer would never be famous. With this bit of insight, I began to design gardens that were camera-friendly and contained points of interest that stood out in photographs.

Rosemary was famous in garden circles, and she loved the limelight which she had certainly earned. Her books were known worldwide, and she had even featured my Virginia garden in one of them, The American Man's Garden. When Rosemary was writing a column for the Times of London, she included my designs. Grateful doesn't begin to describe how I feel. "Oscar…," which sounded like honey being poured when she said it. "Elton …," "His Majesty," and so on. Rosemary loved her stellar clients more than anything – her box of jewels, so to speak.

After Rosemary's death in 2000, her house and gardens were converted into a premiere boutique hotel, and the rich and famous made it a top-notch destination. Rosemary's gardens are the big draw and nothing could be more fitting. Rosemary, who worried about the future of her gardens, must be swooning somewhere among the celestial stars.

Back in Virginia, I began to drop bad habits like a dieter dropping pounds. Purposeful and determined, I wanted to show that Rosemary's guidance hadn't been wasted on someone who was unworthy. I intended to gut it out until I could develop a unique style and fine-tune my garden design skills.

For exposure, I hit the lecture circuit and what I lacked in credentials, I made up for with confidence. I always thought my ideas were brilliant. If they weren't well received, I simply had the wrong audience. Soon I began to wrangle invitations to exhibit at flower shows in Philadelphia, Boston, and New York. After those milestones were reached, I set my sights on the Royal Chelsea Flower Show in London. I had helped Rosemary with an exhibit the year before, and it was her recommendation that led to my participation. Credentials do count, and soon clients began to line up at my door. This time I was ready.

Thanks, Rosemary, for believing in me.

Phillip's Tips

Private gardens should reflect owners' personalities, which is like truth in advertising but expressed with plants. The more of yourself that you put into your garden, the more personal the results will be. The way you dress yourself is certainly a form of self-expression, so why not indulge your garden with the same degree of consideration. Hear that? A good garden can hum, but a great garden can sing. And, I want the Hallelujah Chorus – all stanzas!

The minutes seemed like hours as I fidgeted in the hard pew. Not all Sunday services were as dull as this one-sometimes Reverend Fowler would play along with the organist on his trombone.

But I digress. The drone of the interim pastor's voice was about to render me unconscious when I looked to the side and noticed the colored light streaming in from the stained glass windows. Curlicues of lead divided the panes into various shapes, each filled with liquid color. Light filtered through, depositing the hues on the cushion at my end of the pew. A small rack on the back of the pew held offering envelopes marked for various charities as well as short pencils.

Soon, I was busy copying the window patterns onto the back of the envelopes and adding my flourishes.

As an adult, I would draw on those moments. You might even say that my pattern gardens are a direct result of having gone to church. The Lord does work in mysterious ways.

Phillip's Tips

Making mistakes in the garden is common, even for the experts. However, the experts more often correct them. To avoid pitfalls in my career, I was lucky enough to have Rosemary Verey to guide me.

To avoid pitfalls in *your* garden, do your homework, know your plants, and arrange them wisely with the help of garden experts, garden seminars and books, and especially the internet. Knowledge is power and power, specifically flower power, is beautiful!

BELOW, LEFT TO RIGHT: Greenwich, Connecticut, the Cotswolds of England, the South of France

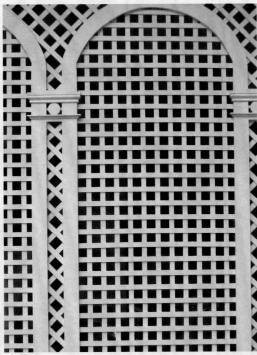

Gardens were my sanctuary when I was growing up in Lexington, Mississippi, and I was surrounded by them. Both of my great aunts, Eloise and Julia, had beautiful gardens. Our house was between the two of theirs, and I spent some of my happiest moments exploring the far corners of their gardens. Aunt Julia had amazing roses, especially 'Perle d'Or' which was introduced in 1884. That beautiful apricot colored rose became the unofficial flower of our family. Every relative has a 'Perle d'Or' rose bush. Eloise, on the other hand, took great pride in her dried catalpa leaf arrangements. I had never seen anything like them before and haven't since.

After Sunday school, my siblings and I were sometimes allowed to escape the church sermon and visit the great aunts. For an hour, we tramped through the dense gardens playing Tarzan and generally running wild. At noon when the church bells rang, we headed home to enjoy a big Sunday feast of fried chicken and various homegrown vegetables. And, of course, lemon ice box pie.

Sometimes after lunch, we took naps but not always inside the house. I can remember lying on my back, eyes closed, and drinking in the smell of the fallen pecan leaves while listening to the blue jays quarreling overhead. Those childhood days were seemingly endless – summer, and no school.

The dried stalks of the finished daylilies stood erect in the long borders flanking Aunt Julia's house. We boys, my brother and I, collected the stalks for use in our Tarzan re-enactments. They made great poison arrows. Reruns of Tarzan came on at one-thirty p.m. every Sunday and by the end of each show, we were quite inspired. Once we built a grass hut out of old hay, which somehow caught fire and nearly burned down the neighbor's house. Lexington, Mississippi, was a fine place back then.

School did inevitably come again, though. Each morning before classes, my best friend, Sammy, and I met at the edge of Mr. Daniel's cornfield for our walk to school. We made our way between the tall rows of mature corn, which formed a great tunnel. At the end of the field was a deep ditch with a large pipe across it. Nearly everyone who attempted to "walk the pipe" fell in. Our expertise at such was an early confidence booster for Sammy and me. Our first period class was "shop" were we learned how to use tools to create things out of wood which meant our next clubhouse was not going to be made out of hay!

My first shop project was to build a portable cage for my poultry enterprise and to attach the crate to the rear of my Honda 50 motorcycle so I could transport some of my birds to the country

where I planned to trade them for other animals as well as plants. My friends, Annie and Jim, whom you will soon meet, had the best creatures I had ever seen – white turkeys, fancy bantams, fantailed pigeons, and speckled guineas. The oddest of all was kept in a crate to itself. Annie said it was half duck and half chicken. Well, to me, it looked like a mangy rooster that had webbed feet. Annie wouldn't part with that thing no matter how I begged, having an idea that when the circus came to town she would get plenty for it.

Back in town, things were a little more ordinary but sweet, none-the-less. Many of my childhood mornings before school were spent with my great aunt Julia. Every morning for breakfast, we had oatmeal with giant globs of butter and lots of brown sugar. Aunt Julia began serving me coffee when I was about seven and I still prefer it to any other refreshment. When Viola, Aunt Julia's housekeeper, brought our trays in, there would always be a small bud vase of 'Perle d'Or' roses. Aunt Julia had an enormous shrub covered in those fragrant soft apricot blooms ten months out of the year.

I was fourteen when Aunt Julia died, and I didn't see how I could possibly survive without her, my grief was so deep. I never fully let her go or, perhaps, she never let me go. I still have dreams about her

Aunt Julia and the herb garden that was inspired by her gingerbread house.

that are so vivid they feel like visits. Aunt Julia's house was festooned in elaborate gingerbread woodwork. The patterns along the porch eaves resembled egrets in flight which I would later copy and use on a large arbor at my Fredericksburg, Virginia, home. In 1992, I built a full size façade of her house replete with a garden of 'Perle d'Or' roses at the Philadelphia Flower Show. My father, who came to see my exhibit, was so pleased. He and his father had both been born in that house.

For my fourteenth birthday, I received my freedom in the form of that Honda 50 motorcycle. I could now go where cars couldn't. Rural dirt roads that narrowed to dirt paths were awfully inviting, and down those byways I discovered a whole new world of old unpainted shacks with tin roofs, which were full of life and excitement. Nearly all of the yards had some sort of garden and many of the porches were lined with old enamelware and nail kegs and were brimming with "exotics" like chicken gizzard coleus and purple wandering jew. I began spending all of my after school time exploring those roads.

One fateful afternoon I came upon what would become my secret magic place. I could just make out two silhouettes on the front porch as I peered through the overhanging limbs of an ancient chinaberry tree. The yard was alive with banty chickens and some were even on the roof of the shack. Already, I had a huge flock of bantams, but I was always on the lookout for beautiful roosters. Some things never change!

That day I met and became fast friends with Annie and Jim. It was 1966. I was fourteen, and they were nearly ninety. A rickety wire fence separated their yard from the narrow dirt road that brought me to their house. That summer, I began to live beyond the confines of my family and realized I'd be just fine if I only had myself to count on. I finally understood that I could develop my own roots far from the family tree, and that there was, indeed, fertile ground outside my own backyard.

Annie and Jim called me "Baby" and were always so glad to see me. They had everything I thought was cool, and both of them smoked pipes! For Christmas that first year, I gave Annie a pipe whose bowl was a bull's head, including horns. When she opened the box, she let out a scream and threw it across the room. A devout believer in curses and spells, Annie was sure I had brought her something possessed. Her bureau was piled high with letters from former Lexington residents who had moved to Chicago. The letters, most of which were brimming with cash, sought the removal of or the casting of spells. My new best friend was a voodoo woman, and I was thrilled!

That winter I spent hours sitting around Annie and Jim's wood stove while chickens roamed free throughout the house looking for scraps. As April approached, I realized that one of the hens that Annie had given me was missing. The poor thing was so beautiful, but she was an outcast. My other chickens, especially the roosters, despised her. Every time the roosters crowed, this hen would also crow. And then all of the chickens would attach her. Soon, she had to roost alone in the mulberry tree.

For days I searched the fields, and the week before Easter I found her, nearly starved to death trying to hatch sixteen infertile eggs. That's how much the roosters hated her. My hen refused to leave the nest even after I removed the eggs, so that afternoon I told Annie about my situation and, as always, she had a plan. Annie took five Muscovey duck eggs that were due to hatch that week and gave them to me. We wrapped the eggs in a warm towel, and I took them to my hen. She covered the eggs, and five days later was the proud mother of five baby ducklings.

On Easter afternoon, I decided to take my hen's hatchlings on an outing. The clover felt soft under my bare feet as I walked up the hill carrying my basket of ducklings. What a beautiful spring day – all fresh and full of promise.

Earlier that morning before Sunday school, my sister and I had our

Architectural details in my Virginia garden in Fredericksburg.

Easter pictures taken in front of the German iris bed – a family ritual.

After I reached the top of the hill, I set my basket down and began making a small corral out of sticks and moss. Once inside their little pen the ducklings began pecking at the white clover flowers. How soft and animated they were, all fluff and curious flat beaks.

The rest of my life has been spent trying to reconstruct those perfect childhood moments when hard edges hadn't yet manifested themselves. Responsibilities were few, and the weight of the world was, well, weightless.

During those early and idyllic times, I began to take notice of nature and all its beauty. The unique fragrance of German iris, the miracle of hatching eggs, the sudden surprise in autumn of the spider lilies, the large sheets of bark that fell from the sycamore trees – all those things enchanted and forever changed me.

As an adult, I would design gardens whose paths would take me to where I liked to walk, and I would use flowers whose fragrance could take me to where my feet could not. In a garden, I wasn't lonely, and I knew nature would never desert me.

Gardening is like comfort food for the soul. Why not recreate the gardens of your childhood by using some of the plants you remember from way back when. My own garden has Aunt Julia's 'Perle d'Or' rose, a seedling oak from my grandfather's yard, and pots of wandering jew which remind me of Annie and Jim. When I see or smell those plants, I am taken back in time to a place that was safe and carefree. Don't we spend most of adult lives chasing that feeling? Your garden can help catch it.

Now, where was I? Oh yes, we'll skip the high school years which involved leaving Lexington and my country life behind. The time was too miserable for words. However, college presented opportunities and freedoms I would relish.

I hadn't wanted to study horticulture when I started college at Mississippi State. I, of course, loved plants and gardening, but to make a career out of it? My father farmed and my brother and I were usually forced to hoe the fields during summer vacation. Well, it was summer, but this was certainly no vacation! I grew to loathe the sight of the fields and the smell of the farm chemicals. Luckily, I got over it.

My university years at Mississippi State University were less than auspicious in terms of grade point average. I rarely attended afternoon lab sessions if the weather was beautiful. Most days were spent sunning myself on the roof of my fraternity house or knocking back a few with my buddies at the local hangouts. My saving grace was the part-time job I had at the MSU greenhouses. Those ancient hulking masses of glass, cinder block, and steam pipes were beautiful to me but seemed as outdated as manual typewriters. Nothing about them was automatic. One of my classes, Greenhouse Management, focused on how these antiques should be efficiently operated. What?! If I hadn't actually worked in those greenhouses, I'm sure I would have slept through class. However, I did pay attention, and I learned how to bleed the air pockets out of hot water pipes, repair glass panes that had slid out of place, and leach the salt out of propagation beds. Many years later, I would be grateful for my experiences at the MSU greenhouses. In 1982, I would buy my very first home in Fredericksburg, Virginia, which would have greenhouses almost identical to those at Mississippi State. I would know exactly how to operate them and would make a good living with them for over twenty years. This I know: knowledge finds its application at some point.

Meanwhile, back at the MSU greenhouses I was feeling a little pensive. I remember gazing out the potting shed window, watching the students heading to and from class and thinking, "Will this be my life – working in the dirt, making next to nothing, and having no social life?" It would be a few years, but the answer to that question would

be beyond my wildest dreams.

After graduating from MSU with a degree in horticulture, I moved to Atlanta with a simple plan – have as much fun as possible until the money ran out. Six months later, I was forced to look for a job.

One afternoon, I was on my way to Zestos to get a Zesto Burger when I noticed this little garden shop in an old house in Ansley Park. The Potted Plant was *the* place to get beautiful pots and plants. The next day I "arrived" on the doorstep dressed for success in bellbottom jeans and 5-inch platform shoes. I fully expected to be hired, and after a brief explanation of 'appropriate attire', I was. Owners Ryan Gainey and Tom Woodham gave me that first post-graduation job in my field, and I was out the chute! I serviced interior plant maintenance accounts for The Potted Plant. Armed with water buckets and a feather duster, I made sure those office plants looked sharp in as little time as possible. After all, it was a sunny day, and I needed to work on my tan.

After a few times of returning to The Potted Plant sunburned from 'interior plant maintenance' tasks, I was given a choice: resign or be fired. After resigning I thought that perhaps I'd like to attend graduate school at the University of Georgia. I mentioned that to my father in Mississippi. I also mentioned that what I REALLY wanted was to move back in with him. The

graduate school money practically flew from his hands!

Once on campus in Athens, Georgia, I signed up for graduate courses in English literature. I loved to read and thought I'd live in a cute house in the country, lift weights, and immerse myself in good books. All of that was fine and dandy until life took quite a different turn.

One day a friend from Atlanta called to suggest that we go to New York for a four-day vacation. All of that reading and weight lifting had begun to wear on me, so I agreed. On the Fourth of July weekend of 1978, I found myself on Fire Island. Life got real interesting in a real hurry. I had intended to be in N.Y. for four days and ended up staying for four years!

On the last day of my four-day vacation, I negotiated with the hotel owner to take care of the grounds for the remainder of the summer in exchange for room and board. The place was transformed by my planters and window boxes.

The next summer I worked the same deal. Finally, "the sporting life" seemed to be within my grasp. I had a summer retreat on Fire Island as well as a Manhattan apartment. After that first summer on Fire Island, I had met another Southerner who had arrived in the Big Apple a few months ahead of me. John was a football player who had attended Texas Tech. Boy

Manhattan, 1979.

did we tear the town up that first winter! Studio 54 was in full swing, and we were young and carefree. I was also unemployed. However, my dear father thought I was still in graduate school in Georgia and continued to send expense checks for another full year. I couldn't have made it otherwise, and I wouldn't have been able to see my rooftop garden creations framed by the Chrysler and Empire State buildings. I am grateful. And, of course, crafty! Sorry, Daddy…

After that first year in Manhattan, John and I moved to a very large apartment in Jackson Heights, Queens. I was about to launch my rooftop garden design business. My first step was to have very expensive business cards printed. The day I picked them up, I attended a cocktail party in Manhattan. At the party, I met the general manager of one of Manhattan's premier hotels and his wife. When the gentleman's wife asked what I did I replied, "Why, I design rooftop gardens," as I handed her one of my new business cards. Lucky timing for me, as it turned out The Essex House was about to be refurbished, and the rooftop gardens needed to be redesigned. My beautiful business card and appropriate attire, did the trick, and I landed an A-list account that would lead to many more.

The subway would no longer do, I thought, as I hailed a taxi, for my triumphant ride back to Jackson Heights, Queens. I burst into our apartment and announced to John, "We have a job!" "What do you mean, we? I already have a job," he exclaimed. Well, what it meant was this: I planned to set up table saws in our dining room and, thanks to my shop class, I was going to make all of the planters myself. And John would, of course, help me.

Soon, I had our dining room practically knee-deep in sawdust, but the planters were turning out beautifully. After installing the Essex House rooftop gardens, I also secured the maintenance account for their upkeep. And another place to maintain my tan! That premiere project put me on the way to the top – the tops of buildings in Manhattan that I would landscape, photograph, and ultimately get published in the *New York Times*.

Just when I thought that all foolishness was over and that my gardening career was about to bloom, some more wild oat seeds blew my way. While installing the Essex House project, I went down to the street to use the pay phone. (Remember, this was 1979.) I had on appropriate attire for gardening – cutoff jeans, no shirt, and work boots. I was also filthy from digging holes and planting trees. Well, this nicely dressed lady begins to circle the phone booth while I'm talking. I finally got irritated and said, "I'll be through in an MINUTE!" She grabbed my arm and said, "Oh, I just wanted to talk to you about modeling. Would you come up to my office (she gestured to a nearby doorway) for a photo test?" And so began my amazing but short-lived modeling career. The one thing I did like was being invited to every A-list party and club opening. It was unimaginable at the time, but my gardening career would soon land me at more parties and galas than seemed possible. And for better reasons than just being a pretty face. In the meantime, I was having to juggle my plant maintenance schedules with my erratic photo shoots for the agency.

There were three other models at the agency who looked a lot like me. However, no one could design gardens that looked even remotely like mine. The agency didn't understand why I quit showing up for bookings. They should have looked up because I was high above them installing beautiful gardens.

When Christmas rolled around my second year in Manhattan, I decided to go home for the holidays. I intended to spread the glad tidings of my success to anyone who would listen. When I lived in Mississippi both Thanksgiving and Christmas were spent at the deer camp. All the men in the family hunted, and I was no exception, but this particular Christmas was to be spent at my mother's parents' home in Crystal Springs. We were all about

Memama's cooking! As I reached for my second piece of chicken, I began my story about designing rooftop gardens for my extremely wealthy clients in Manhattan. After a few moments, Memama put on her most Baptist of smiles and proclaimed, "Now Phil, you know money won't buy happiness." Without blinking I replied, "And Memama, poverty won't buy anything." I still stand by that.

A few years after Memama passed away, I visited my 95-year-old granddaddy who was still in their house. This was my first visit since Memama had died. Dorothy, his devoted housekeeper, informed me that Granddaddy had a surprise for me. He made sure I wasn't disappointed. After asking if I were ready, he proceeded to sing every verse of "Turkey in the Straw" while dancing a jig. I was floored. Granddaddy had always been so strict and business-like. The month before Memama died, she had suddenly burst into song, singing "I Love Paris" from beginning to end. I had never heard her sing before. And I had certainly never seen Granddaddy dance. I saw Granddaddy's performance as a sign, and I tried my best to memorize every aspect of that visit, which would be the last.

After lunch, which felt weird without Memama, Granddaddy and I took a walk in the backyard. Memama's pink and prickly rose bush was still in flower, and I

winced just a little at that painful reminder of a childhood biking mishap. It was early December and the paperwhite narcissuses were blooming as they always did this time of year. I picked one and handed it to Granddaddy, remarking how sweet it smelled. As he brought the narcissus to his nose, he looked at me and said, "I didn't know they were fragrant." Amazing.

After four years in N.Y., it was time to go. I longed for sunsets and sunrises as well as trees and birds. And off I went to begin yet another chapter, which would prove to be the longest and best so far.

Briefly, I lived in Washington, D.C., before settling in Fredericksburg, Virginia, where I would remain for twenty-three years. Each week I took Amtrak from D.C. to Penn. Station in Manhattan because I didn't have any work in Washington yet and had to continue my interior plant maintenance contracts in N.Y. in order to survive. Soon, however, I would land contracts in D.C., which would dwarf those in New York. Meanwhile, I boarded the train each week with my trusty feather duster and water buckets. Who else but Phillip Watson would commute five hours each way to water office plants?!

OPPOSITE: 'Winter Gem' boxwood arranged in an "anchored" parterre in a sea of crushed shells.

18

Coleus

While on one of those trips to Manhattan, I began looking through real estate brochures I had picked up at my bank and just as the train approached the Baltimore station, I found my dream home. I had skipped over it the first time because I could see houses on either side of it, which made me think the property was too small. However, the description stated that the house was on eight acres and had four big glass greenhouses! I was so excited that I got off the train in Baltimore and boarded the next southbound train for Fredericksburg, Virginia. I was afraid someone else would beat me to it. That afternoon at the real estate office I put in an offer, and in a week the house and "Wine's Greenhouses" were mine. And there they were – ancient greenhouses much like those at Mississippi State. I knew just how to operate them and with the loving and helpful guidance of my surrogates, Mr. and Mrs. Wine, I was able to produce a successful crop of poinsettias that first year. If my crop had failed, I would have been ruined since I had spent everything I had acquiring the property. I didn't trust the alarm system, which was supposed to alert me if the heat went off in the greenhouses, so I set up a cot among the poinsettias. I figured I'd wake up if it got cold. It all turned out fine, and my nursery was up and running.

I simply loved producing plants in the greenhouses. This was certainly a far cry from rooting coleus plants in Coke bottles in the kitchen window.

Rare and heirloom plants were my focus. I couldn't possibly compete with the large volume greenhouses, so I had to specialize, deciding to grow plants that couldn't be found anywhere else. If you wanted those plants, I was the only one who had them, and because of this steady supply of unusual plants, the gardens I designed were unique. As such, I simply had no competition. All of the other gardens were full of the usual red geraniums, pink petunias, and orange marigolds while I surprised everyone with golden cuphea from South Africa, variegated Japanese iris, and yellow-berried nandina.

After being open to the public for a number of years, I decided to produce only plants for my garden design clients and soon I was taking truckloads of annuals and perennials all over Virginia and up to the District of Columbia. I even supplied a project in Jackson, Mississippi. But the scope of my business was about to change.

In late summer of 1994, I received two calls from Greenwich, Connecticut. Neither of the two ladies knew one another but they had both read an article in *Southern Accents* magazine about me and my gardens in Virginia. Both wanted consultations, which I was able to arrange for the same weekend. Patricia Chadwick wanted a day long consultation for her husband, John, who was an avid and accomplished gardener. The other call came from Alease Fisher. Upon meeting Alease, I was enchanted. If Glenda the Good Witch had landed in the garden beside me I wouldn't have noticed.

Alease and Patricia became friends of mine, and I had the pleasure of watching their children grow into young adults during the time I was developing their gardens. And so began my chapter of garden design in Greenwich, Connecticut. I was luckier than I knew at the time.

Over the years, I had seen many people in my field fail during hard economic times, and I had no intention of being one of them. Working in Greenwich, Connecticut, somewhat insulated me from the ups and the downs of a volatile economy. Those industrious and clever folks in Greenwich would surely be the last ones to run out of money!

On my 50th birthday, Alease took me to France for a series of lavish parties at Versailles. Elaborate parterres dotted the landscape, punctuated with astonishing fountains and waterworks. That first evening we were treated to a display of fireworks over the reflecting pools outside the orangerie whose edges were lined with Versailles boxes full of various citrus trees. Just as Alease and I entered the Hall of Mirrors, we were photographed. The next week our picture filled a half page in the *Chicago Tribune* with a caption which described us as an example of the glamour that was on display at the American Friends of Versailles Ball!

Everything Rosemary Verey had told me was coming true. My career, like hers, had also become my social life. Countless other parties preceded the Versailles event, and countless others were to follow. Foolish was replaced by Fabulous who would be joined by Clarity much later in my life. But that's another book…

My television career as a garden expert began quite by accident. While on a lecture tour of the U.S. with *Horticulture* magazine, I met a young woman, Anita Nelson, who managed a large aquatic garden center in Texas. She and I became friends, and shortly after the tour ended, she asked me to give a couple of lectures at her place of business. An old buddy from my Manhattan days, Elvin McDonald, was living in Houston at the time. I invited him to my talks at the garden center so we could get caught up. Elvin had just been made editor of *Traditional Home* magazine and would soon be relocating to Des Moines. And this is where it gets interesting. It seems that two garden shows for PBS were to be filmed the afternoon of my lectures. The film crew was there, but somehow the hosts never arrived so I was drafted to fill in. The two segments, one on water gardening and the other on bog gardening, went well. After the filming, Elvin told me he had a business associate who was looking for a new spokesperson to sell plants on live TV and would I be interested. My eyes were so far out on stems, you could have picked them! Anyway, kind and generous Elvin sent off tapes of my PBS shows (The New Garden) to his friend who interviewed and ultimately hired me. That friend of Elvin's is Jim Freid to whom I am eternally grateful for giving me a chance. Over the years, Jim and I have traveled to nurseries throughout the U.S. as well as England and South Africa. We continue to be on the lookout for the latest in plant discoveries as well as long-lost heirloom varieties. Being in front of the camera and speaking to millions about gardening is certainly a lofty perch compared to that old potting shed at Mississippi State. And the view is a lot better.

Clipped Patterns

The gardens of France and England pretty much set me on fire. I couldn't wait to try my hand at pattern gardens. I loved sketching and relished the thought of working with a living canvas. Success would hinge on proper scale and detail, appropriate plant selection, and meticulous maintenance.

Parterres and other pattern gardens are the large canvasses created by the organization of clipped plants. Quite simply, the plants are used as architecture and may actually echo portions of nearby structures. Hedge tops are level, corners are plumb and at perfect 90° angles. A wooly or crooked parterre with blurred lines looks like a derelict building – or someone who doesn't go to the gym!

Phillip's Tips

Electric shears may be used carefully to rough-cut topiaries and to shape shrubs. Always fine tune with hand shears. Never hard prune evergreen shrubbery after Labor Day.

What makes a pattern garden special is the precision in which it was constructed and, more importantly, the precision in which it was maintained. When maintained at the highest level, a pattern garden becomes a magical marvel, especially when frosted or dusted by snow in winter.

Most of my successful designs happen in a hurry, and I can create pattern garden plans in a matter of minutes. However, refining those plans takes a bit longer. Scale and proportion aren't just aesthetic elements, and plants must have room enough to grow and mature without compromising the crispness of the pattern. Choosing the right plant for any situation is critical, but pattern gardens, especially, need perfectly suited plants. There is simply – literally – no room for error.

If you intend for a hedge to be no taller than four feet, do not attempt to use plants that mature at ten feet. If you have a size eight foot, does it make sense to buy size four shoes? Whether you are selecting foundation plants that won't cover your windows or boxwood edging that won't overwhelm your pathways, do a little homework so you can avoid of lot of yard work.

After giving a lecture on pattern gardens and their maintenance, I always hear the whining: "Well, we just can't get good help." "They cut down the camellias; can you believe it?" "The

BELOW AND LEFT: Datura (Angel Trumpet).

25

yardman never came back." Of course, he didn't come back. He was being paid less than a ditch digger, and he had no idea what a camellia is. Lesson #1: Don't expect a skillful result if you hire unskilled labor. It's ok to negotiate a fair price, but being cheap usually ends up being expensive. And while we're on the subject of unskilled labor, let me get this off my chest. Please don't cancel the haircut appointments for your children because you happen to own some scissors. Take a look at the topiaries your yardman created before he ran off. And Mama, I'm still mad about my hair!

Patterned and clipped gardens, like all gardens, should have a pleasing balance of discipline and whimsy. My parterre designs may be carefully laid out and perfectly trimmed, but the patterns flow and evoke a sense of humor. All work and no play makes for dull day, so have fun with your garden. After all, wouldn't you rather attend a garden party than a garden seminar?

Inspiration for my pattern garden designs comes from all sorts of places. Once, I saw an exquisite bench in France whose design covered all the bases. The seat portion was a diagonal grid pattern – very mathematical and disciplined, but the back of the bench was a flourish of arabesques and intertwining arcs – a perfect balance of discipline and whimsy. Pattern designs can be inspired by or directly lifted from the designs of fabric, windows, paving, benches, tile-work, and jewelry.

After my patterns are completed and properly scaled on paper, I make several copies. Once the site for my proposed parterre has been prepared and smoothed, I arrive with these tools: marking paint, tape measure, stakes and strings, the plan, and a large thermos of coffee. Mocha java always gets me going, and as my granddaddy used to say, "I like my coffee to speak with authority!"

Once I am fully simulated, I stake out the four corners of my plan to create a box within which to lay out my planting scheme.

If your pattern is a balanced rectilinear design, it is easy to measure and mark with your tape measure, stakes, and strings. The marking paint comes later after your grids have been established. Once the stakes and strings are in place, simply paint over them to transfer your design to the soil surface. Take a good look at the results. I often have to simplify mine at this

point. What looked perfect on paper doesn't always work in the field, so revise if necessary to avoid being married to a mistake.

It is critical that your plants aren't cramped. If the design is too tight, your pattern will disappear as the plants mature. Remember, plant maturity isn't just about height; the ultimate width of your plants is just as key.

Once you are satisfied with your design, you may remove the stakes and strings and begin to dig the plant trenches along the painted lines. If you are using one- gallon boxwoods, for example, make the trenches a few inches wider than the pots. This spacing allows room to maneuver the plants within the trenches to create a clean and continuous line. After all of the plants are in place – the side branches of each plant should slightly touch its neighbor's – backfill the trenches without burying the root crowns of the plants, and firm the soil around and between the plants before thoroughly watering. On the following day check to see if the soil has settled. You may need to add soil to some areas. Adding 2-3 inches of mulch (your choice of type) will provide an instant, finished look, and the mulch prevents surface drying and discourages weed growth.

OPPOSITE: American Cranberry Viburnum (Viburnum trilobum)

BELOW LEFT: Boxwood parterre which was featured in Frank Oz's 2004 movie "The Stepford Wives." BELOW: Alease and Phillip in the Hall of Mirrors at Versailles, France in 2002.

Finally, you may give your pattern garden a smoothing trim and, Voila! You have a garden that is beautiful year-round.

If your pattern isn't based on a grid and has more curves than corners, you may take a painterly approach as you layout your design. This sort of pattern works best if you have a "good eye" since curves are difficult to plot mathematically. After completing your excellent free-hand layout, stand atop a tall ladder to see whether or not your pattern is pleasing. If you have a helper, one person can direct from the top of the ladder while the other adjusts the pattern.

Never begin planting until you have set your plants out on top of the painted lines. The pattern may look perfect, but lining out your plants will show you exactly how it will look after planting. If you are satisfied, it's time to get your shovel and get busy.

The interiors of your finished pattern garden needn't be filled with anything except mulch unless you subscribe to the theory that more is actually more. I'm from the South where we like to say, "It isn't done until it's overdone!" Anyway, I try to embellish all things in my life – especially gardens.

Possible candidates for filling your parterres include low annuals and ground covers. Neither choice should exceed half the height of the clipped pattern. Lower, cleaner, and more permanent fillers include crushed limestone, oyster shell, lava rock, and pea gravel. Even if the interiors are only covered in mulch, lay down plastic sheets within the compartments before trimming the plants which makes cleanup easier, and the surfaces will remain pristine.

A pattern garden is only as brilliant as its maintenance, and smooth surfaces on tightly clipped plants are beautiful as well as sturdy. There is nothing like an ice storm or wet snow to point out poorly pruned or neglected plants. Often after such storms, I see boxwoods and hollies laid open and split which is largely due to poor, infrequent, or non-existent pruning. Proper trimming, if begun when plants are young, promotes an inner network of multi-branched limbs that can withstand harsh weather conditions. Consider trimming your clipped forms as often as you get a haircut. Surely, you get more than one haircut a year. Or perhaps a parterre that looks like a haystack works for you. It is what it is. However, some may ask, "But, what is it?"

If you don't have space for a parterre but love clipped and shaped plants, you might try your hand at topiaries. Individual plants can be pruned into patterns and kept in the ground or used as container plantings but ready-made topiaries of spiraled junipers, standard tree roses, and poodled hollies and boxwoods are commonly available. These fancy shapes are real eye-catchers when used as pairs flanking a gate entrance or doorway.

Other clipped forms for small gardens include tall hedges and foundation plantings. Although these clipped plants don't require the higher maintenance of the parterres, they should be kept smooth and free of gaps.

There are many ideas out there about how to trim plants within a clipped garden. To save time I very carefully rough-cut my plants with power shears. Be conservative, and don't try to accomplish a finish-cut with these tools. Instead, go over the plants with hand shears to complete their haircuts so the results will be refined and won't display the creases that power tools often yield.

Nothing in a garden causes jaws to drop as much as the sight of a pattern or topiary garden. Prepare to be the talk of the town, except this time it won't be embarrassing!

ABOVE: Boxwood pattern with crushed sea shells.
OPPOSITE: Crushed sea shells.

"Coffee is served!"
Make certain garden
helpers are supplied
with plenty of water
while they work.
If you'd like speedier
results, mocha java
should do the trick!

OPPOSITE: Immaculately trimmed at ten
feet tall, 'Blue Ice' Arizona cypress.

40

Roses

All week long, I rode up and down my grandparents' driveway on my hand-me-down bicycle. One day, Memama declared that if I could learn to ride without training wheels, she would buy a brand new bicycle for me. That afternoon, she and I went down to Biggs Hardware Store to take a look. Oh my, the bicycles were all so beautiful and shiny – not rusty like mine.

The next day my lessons began. Somehow, Granddaddy had managed to pry the training wheels off the old bike, and it was ready for a test run. With a great push, Memama sent me off on my wild ride through the backyard. I felt pretty confident until I saw the large rosebush directly in front of me and it was at that moment that I realized I didn't know how to turn.

After I picked myself up, all scratched and embarrassed, Memama put her hands on her hips and said, "I'll bet you won't do that again!" Well, I didn't end up in the thorn bush again, but I did get my new bicycle as well as a new respect for roses!

Phillip's Tips

Never hard prune roses in autumn. Wait to prune in late winter or early spring when new buds are just emerging.

PREVIOUS PAGE: Rosa 'The Alnwick Rose', a David Austin selection. OPPOSITE: Rosa 'Perle d'Or', introduced in 1884.

OPPOSITE: Rosa 'Pearly Gates'
climbing on an arbor.

A garden isn't a garden without at least one rose bush. If you've never grown roses before, try one of the easier varieties. Once you have mastered that, you may want to begin a collection. Starting with a large rose garden before knowing roses is a disastrous idea. Do your homework, make logical selections based on your knowledge, and refuse to be seduced by the pictures in the catalogues. Some roses, like trophy wives, are high maintenance, although a little arm-candy for your garden isn't a bad thing as long as you understand the hidden costs.

When starting small, why not consider mini-roses? They have always been a favorite with gardeners and work in a variety of situations from in-ground beds to window boxes to container plantings. Rainbows of colors are available which include single and double forms, cascading and upright varieties, and bicolors and solids. The name "mini-rose" refers to the size of the blooms and foliage, not the bush. Some mini-roses easily reach four feet in height and width while others are more compact. Always check tags for the mature sizes of all plants you purchase so they can be situated properly in your garden.

Old rose varieties, which often only bloom once, are certainly more fragrant than most of the new hybrids. An exception is the new class of roses being offered by David Austin. The David Austin

LEFT: Knockout roses, pink and red. BELOW: Rosa rugosa. BOTTOM: Rosa 'American Pillar.'

roses are bred to look and smell like antique varieties but without their typical problems. Fewer diseases and longer blooming periods put these roses at the top of my list.

If you have a "brown thumb," however, the Knockout series of roses will provide great satisfaction and a sense of accomplishment. The flowers of the Knockout roses are smaller and less fragrant than the David Austins, but they never stop blooming and are the lowest maintenance of any roses I have ever grown, which is why they are frequently used in commercial settings in less than ideal conditions. The reds and pinks are available as singles and doubles and perform the best for me, although I also like the new golden variety, Sunny Knockout.

The number one problem that roses face is blackspot. Removing old foliage and spent blossoms from the bushes and the ground beneath them is essential. Avoid overhead watering, particularly after sundown, by employing a drip irrigation system or a carefully aimed hose since wet foliage encourages diseases when night temperatures are above seventy degrees Fahrenheit.

For gardens with limited space, try climbing roses, which are easily trained along fences, attached to downspouts, or woven through arbors. A climbing rose can produce up to ten times the amount of flowers per square foot of bed space than a hybrid tea rose bush. And you thought you didn't have room for roses!

If you have had good luck with mini-roses, guess what? There are climbing mini-roses available with the same profusion of blossoms that are produced practically non-stop. A bed of regular mini-roses is made even more dramatic by the addition of climbing mini-roses on the fence or wall behind it. For additional interest, clamoring clematis vines may be allowed to intertwine with any of the climbing roses. Clematis and roses are beautiful companions and enjoy a peaceful co-existence.

Now, for a morality lesson; please pay attention. Titillating pictures in rose catalogues are basically plant pornography. It's all very exciting to peruse; just think twice about what you bring home. Study your short list of rose candidates and make selections based on beauty and merit. Know your limitations whether they are physical, financial, intellectual, or…moral!

A rose garden can be your best friend or your worst enemy. It all depends on how both of you behave.

And, as I discovered while learning to ride a bicycle at Memama's house, a rose bush sounds mighty nice until you find yourself in the middle of one!

Phillip's Tips

If you hate to spray climbing roses for blackspot, use one-time bloomers which perform before blackspot season. Plant clematis vines with the roses to provide a second but carefree show of flowers.

Hydrangeas

Hydrangeas are always near the top of the list of most loved flowers. Nearly everyone's grandmother had hydrangeas, but not all of those grandmothers were good gardeners. One reason they succeeded is because hydrangeas are fairly easy to grow.

The hydrangeas of my grandmother's day have been improved upon considerably. Hers, which were mop-heads, bloomed only once and sometimes not even that. The old-fashioned varieties set bud exclusively on old wood in the fall, and if a harsh winter followed, most of the buds could freeze, resulting in lots of foliage in spring but no hydrangea blooms.

Spectacular new varieties of mop-head hydrangeas are now available, and they bloom on new and old wood. Even, after a harsh winter, if the old buds die, new buds will take their place in spring.

Phillip's Tips

For blue hydrangea blossoms, pour a cup of granular aluminum sulfate around the root zone of each established mophead or lacecap hydrangea bush on April Fools Day. Fertilize with a formula for acid-loving plants.

Pink blooms are produced by using a cup of dolomitic lime and 25-10-10 fertilizer. Water in thoroughly.

OPPOSITE: Hydrangea 'Pee Gee' in August.

LEFT AND BELOW: Hydrangea 'Annabelle'. BOTTOM: Hydrangea 'Blushing Bride'.

'Endless Summer', 'Blushing Bride', and 'Penny Mac' are three of the best reblooming hydrangeas and are particularly favored by those in colder regions because of their spring bounce-back.

Plants that bloom only once don't usually earn their keep in the smaller gardens many of us have. The reblooming hydrangeas are perfect company for reblooming daylilies as well as reblooming German iris. Choose your plants carefully, and you will never be without flowers.

Hydrangeas have many uses but none quite as clever as my next story will illustrate. When my friends and I were children we were generally inspired by everything we saw on television, and it didn't end with Tarzan! Once, after watching South Pacific, I decided that my best girlfriend, Betsy Alice, would make a beautiful island girl. We constructed a skirt for her out of daylily leaves. And since we didn't have the requisite coconut halves for her top, we used blue hydrangea mop-heads. Betsy Alice was simply stunning, and for once we received applause instead of spankings!

Hydrangea mop-heads are either blue or pink, depending on the soil pH. The more acid the soil, the bluer the blooms. For pink, an alkaline soil does the trick. If your pH is right in the middle, the blooms may be lavender or purple. This color-change works on mop-head as well as lacecap hydrangeas. But before we get too far down the hydrangea highway, I'd like to tell a Tinsel Town story about the "clever" use of blue hydrangeas.

Location scouts arrived at my friend, Alease Fisher's house, searching for movie sites to shoot the remake of *The Stepford Wives*. The scouts were especially keen on finding properties that had clipped and CONTROLLED gardens. Well, the movie WAS about controlling those wives. And what could be more controlled than my Versailles-inspired central parterre in front of Alease's house! The film actually featured an aerial shot of that pattern garden.

After selecting the property and setting the shoot date, the set designer arrived for a tour of the grounds. He wanted to know the names of all of the plants that might possibly be in the movie shots. As we approached the front of the house, the gentleman asked what the vines were that had climbed almost to the roof. "Why, those are climbing hydrangeas. You should see them when they are in bloom." That was all I said, and I never thought about it again until I returned to the property for filming.

Upon arrival on the filming date, I was astonished. Although it was late September, the garden had been made to look like late spring. Even fake wisteria blooms had been wired to the real vines which covered a newly constructed pergola. The book club scene would be filmed there.

As I rounded the corner to the front of the house, I saw that the asphalt drive had been covered in crushed stone for a more rustic look, *and* the climbing hydrangea vines had been smothered with huge blue mop-heads. Then I remembered: the set designer had never asked me about the climbing hydrangea blooms, which are ALWAYS white. The entire front of the house was truly a "Rhapsody in Blue." Ah, Hollywood…

The only white hydrangea that is color-changing is the reblooming mop-head, 'Blushing Bride', which opens snow white and changes to blue or pink per soil conditions.

Although hydrangeas aren't terribly particular about soil conditions, they prefer their beds to be moist but well drained and rich in humus and compost. Apply three to four inches of shredded mulch to help maintain even moisture and prevent surface drying. Hydrangeas do their best in areas that are suitable for dogwoods, redbuds, and azaleas – the edges of woodland, beneath high canopy trees or eastern exposure. Also like the dogwood, hydrangeas will wilt to show they are thirsty. They aren't dying and will quickly bounce back after a through watering.

Hydrangea shrubs are so nicely formed that they may be used as stand-alone plants. A mature hydrangea shrub has a rounded habit and will bloom from top to bottom, never looking leggy. This is particularly enhanced when reblooming varieties are utilized. Because mop-head hydrangea blooms are so large, they are noticeable even from far away. I prefer to situate my hydrangeas some distance from the house since they drop their leaves in winter. When planted against a fence, the bare stems will quietly blend in.

As spring approaches, wait until green buds emerge before doing any trimming, removing only the dead tips and the occasional dead limb. Even the most ragged-looking hydrangea will form a rounded habit after fully leafing-out. Remember when Mama got carried away when cutting your hair? Restraint, restraint…

OPPOSITE: Lacecap hydrangea.

Phillip's Tips

Never prune hydrangeas after Labor Day to avoid removing many of next year's flower buds. An exception to that rule is Hydrangea 'Annabelle' which may be cut back as far as fifteen inches above the ground on April 15th.

Phillip's Tips

White blooming hydrangeas such as 'Pee Gee', 'Annabelle', and the climbing varieties are perpetually white except when they fade to pinkish rust at the end of the season. No amount of acid fertilizer will turn them blue.

Fall Glory

As fall approaches, the blooms of the statuesque 'Pee Gee' hydrangeas take on a beautiful pinkish copper hue. They may be cut and dried at this time to enjoy in arrangements throughout the winter.

One of the first trees to show fall color are the Japanese maples which are extremely long-lived and sturdy. Japanese maples are even beautiful after all the leaves have dropped, and the weeping forms resemble wire sculptures.

My friend, Alease, has a beautiful and ancient weeping Japanese maple in her front garden. When I first saw it, it reminded me of one of my childhood clubhouses, and before I knew it, I had crawled inside. Its limbs, which reached all the way to the ground, formed a perfect canopy. The cool fall nights had transformed the once burgundy foliage into glowing honey, and once inside, I was quite hidden. The sunshine illuminated the outer shell, and I could see the filigreed patterns of the finely dissected maple leaves silhouetted against the blue autumn sky.

"And meanwhile, summer turns to fall.
Roses bloom and fade; life goes on.
You can measure it all by the difference it made."

"Meanwhile" by singer/songwriter Mac McAnally

Phillip's Tips

Keep fish ponds free of fallen leaves in autumn. The fallen foliage can sour the water and kill the fish. A mesh of nylon or chicken wire is a good barrier as long as it is cleaned off every few days.

Durable and reliable, Japanese maples are among the most sought-after of ornamental trees, and their beauty typically outshines all others. Virtually pest free, these special trees require no spraying or trimming.

Autumn is one of the finest seasons of the year when temperatures are most comfortable, and the garden possesses a quiet beauty. It's quiet, because the children have finally gone back to school!

Every fall I typically spend a month in Aspen. Upon my arrival in early September, the gardens are popping with late-season color. 'Stargazer' oriental lilies, 'Autumn Joy' sedum, garlands of purple clematis, great stands of hollyhocks, and sweet peas greet me as I ride my bicycle through some of the older neighborhoods. I never get a car, preferring instead to hike and bike armed with coat and camera. The cool night temperatures may chill me, but they also heighten the fall foliage hues. The flowers respond to the lower temperatures as well and are at their most vivid zeniths.

Aspen, of course, gets its name from the trees that cover its mountainsides, and by early October, the white trunked trees are a rich golden yellow. Unlike the multi-colored trees of the Northeast, Aspen's autumn canvas is nearly exclusively awash in yellow.

My parents loved Aspen so much that they spent their honeymoon there at the historic Hotel Jerome. Maybe that's why I feel such a connection to the place. After all, I am their oldest child…

For years, my father attempted to grow aspen trees in Mississippi, but to no avail. Although we can't have the electric yellows of Aspen in the deep South, we can enjoy the similarly golden glow of ginkgoes and the creamy white barks of native sycamores and 'Heritage' river birches.

Autumn is the best time to set out new trees and shrubs and to restock perennial borders. Early fall plantings develop strong root systems long before they begin to bud or leaf-out in spring. Permanent plantings done in spring have the double task of root and foliage production. Fall planting will increase the survival rate.

The cooler temperatures of fall make gardening tasks less arduous, and the mild conditions are also welcomed by recently installed plants which can relax in their new locations, put down fresh

BELOW LEFT: Sternbergia lutea. BELOW: Acer freemanii 'Autumn Blaze'. BOTTOM: Acer palmatum, weeping red form. OPPOSITE: Chrysanthemum 'Sheffield' and lambs ear.

roots, and prepare for winter. One good and thorough watering after planting should be enough to take them through the dormant period, especially if three inches of mulch is applied.

I shop for trees and shrubs in autumn the way most people shop for annuals in spring, but instead of looking for particular flower colors, I look for fall leaf color. Many trees and shrubs are being bred for increased autumn brilliance – even in the deep South. As such, one may create garden drama from the earth to the sky by using shrubs and trees that color-up as winter approaches. Interesting stems, bark, and fruit add dimension to the garden even after the autumn leaves have been raked. Some plants produce beautiful fruit, which persists well into winter, providing forage for resident birds.

Plants that produce fall fruit certainly enhance the habitat qualities of a garden, but true habitat gardening is a year-round endeavor. "Why are you cutting down the coneflowers?" a gardening friend once asked. "Because, they are finished," I replied. I was quickly informed that the goldfinches were most certainly not finished and had been waiting all summer for those seed-heads to ripen in autumn. So began my understanding of habitat gardening and all the riches it would bring to my life.

BELOW: Euonymus alatus 'Compacta' hedge.

There were all sorts of creatures in my garden, but I didn't know why they were there, and so I began to pay attention. The caterpillars that annually devour the fennel emerge as swallowtail butterflies in late summer and early fall. My resident mockingbirds stay in my garden long past summer because of the fall-fruiting lantana and the ripe red berries of the dogwoods. Other esteemed guests include the hummingbirds who buzz like bees around the salvia because I don't use toxic chemicals, a multitude of frog species who serenade me until first frost because I built a bog garden and the gray fox family who took up residence in an old groundhog tunnel as if to bless my efforts.

Of all the garden guests, I must say the mockingbirds are my favorite. They never abandon me, and we have a long-term relationship ("LTR," you cyber-geeks!). The mockingbirds are the guardians of my garden and, well, I just love them.

Once, when I lived in Virginia, I was out by my pool when I heard a bunch of birds making a fuss on the other side of the fence. I went to inspect and saw sparrows flying in and out of a large holly hedge. As I stepped towards the hedge, a mockingbird flew down at my feet and just stood there. I looked down, and that's when I saw the snake – all six feet of it. I won't tell what happened next except I was grateful for the mockingbird and the sparrows were grateful for me.

While on the lookout for snakes, be sure to notice these reliable fall bloomers – the golden-yellow and crocus-like sternbergia, deep purple asters, watermelon colored spider lilies, apricot-hued 'Sheffield' chrysanthemums, and, my favorite, the reblooming German iris ('Immortality', which is white, is the best variety).

As autumn settles in, drink in the cool fresh air and take time to notice the things that are strictly autumnal. Fall needn't consist of leaf piles and caved-in Jack-o'-lanterns. Honor the season with brilliant new plantings and fresh gardening ideas.

BELOW, LEFT TO RIGHT: 'Autumn Joy' sedum, Lycoris radiata spider lily and 'Hella Lacy' aster for Monarch butterflies.

Winter Wonder

"Gosh, it's quiet," I thought when I first awakened. My dog, Petey, was standing at the end of the bed staring out the window. It was still well before sunrise, but my bedroom seemed brighter than the time indicated. Petey, my six-month-old whippet, was looking at something he had never seen before. SNOW, and lots of it! Overnight we had received an unpredicted blanket that was 6" deep, and it was still falling – sticking to everything in my Virginia garden.

Phillip's Tips

Remember, evergreen shrubbery that hasn't been trimmed properly will look like a wooly mess in winter and may even collapse under the weight of ice or snow. Properly trimmed and maintained shrubs and hedges develop tight networks of branches that can withstand harsh winter challenges.

As the first frosts of the season settle over the garden, the clipped forms stand out like sculpture. Blue shadows fill the indentations of the spiraled boxwood hedge producing a zebra-like effect with frost on the raised portions. At this time of year, which is typically devoid of those bells and whistles called flowers, light quietly takes center stage.

If you have planned your garden carefully, there will be more to enjoy in the winter than the pictures in the plant catalogues. Once all of the leaves have dropped, hopefully revealing interesting bark and winter fruits, make a good effort to clear debris from the garden. After re-edging the flower beds, apply a fresh layer of mulch. Crisp and clean beds complement the garden, and it's just hard to appreciate interesting bark and winter fruit when there are small tumbleweeds in the same picture. Winter garden interest is subtle stuff and what would have been a minor distraction in the full-blown garden of the summer, is a glaring blemish in winter. Cleanliness, cleanliness…

OPPOSITE: Christmas wreath on my front door in Atlanta.

With leaves gone, it's time to inspect deciduous trees and shrubs for crisscrossing and damaged or cracked limbs. Also, check for leaf compost that may have settled into the interiors of shrubbery – especially boxwood and azaleas. As compost builds inside the branches, it creates a situation similar to planting too deep, and rot and disease will come a-knockin'!

The perfect maintenance that you performed on your clipped plants is now evident. Just look how beautiful the frost is on the smooth surfaces of the hollies and the boxwoods – like icing on a cake!

To ramp-up interest in the winter garden, consider this: Evergreen foliage needn't be green. My dear friend Rosemary Verey told me many years ago that the difference between a good garden and a great garden was the foliage. She utilized evergreen plants, which were variegated, golden, blue, and silver. Green is certainly nice, but in the depths of winter can appear almost black. Colorful foliage lifts the spirits on those gray winter days when all of those flowers you thought were so beautiful in summer are nowhere to be found.

When the holidays roll around, clip some of the interesting foliage for mantle decorations and wreath making. How clever – a winter cutting garden!

I know your feet are getting cold, but don't go inside just yet. What about the pots? Terra cotta (clay) pots are particularly susceptible to freezing and thawing whether they are the cheap standard variety or the super expensive Italian type. Move them to a shed or garage so they won't fall apart, emptying them first.

Now that the pots are safely stored, why not bring in the garden furniture. Winter is the perfect time to clean and repaint those items before spring sneaks up on you. Don't forget to wash and store the cushions too.

At least a third of my container plantings are in place year-round and contain permanent displays of hardy evergreens while some pots are periodically replanted to suit the season. Synthetic resin containers are lightweight, easy to move, and frost-proof, but for a more glamorous look, try the hard-fired and glazed Malaysian pottery that comes in a variety of shapes, colors, and sizes. I have never seen one crack from winter temperatures, and they are stunning even when left empty.

In milder areas of the country, winter container plantings of ornamental cabbages and kales, pansies and Dusty Miller provide bright spots at doorways, on terraces, and even along driveways.

Life is too short, and winter is too long to endure ugliness for even a moment. Plan your winter garden carefully, and it will stand out like a beacon of hope that spring will, indeed, come again.

Phillip's Tips

Forget to cut your perennials back in the fall? If they remain, they need to be clipped to three or four inches before adding fresh mulch.

Garden Seating

Spring finally arrives, and it's time to bring the containers and garden furniture out of the garage. Aren't you glad to see un-cracked pots, clean cushions, and sturdy benches? Pick a few daffodils to reward yourself. You are sitting in the catbird seat!

Often fashion trumps function, which can create quite a slippery slope. Good designs and good intentions should yield good results. It is all right to have a folly in your garden, but it isn't all right for your garden to be a folly.

Phillip's Tips

Garden furniture can be made of many different materials. Wooden benches made of teak, cypress, or cedar last much longer and are sturdier than their cheaper cousins fabricated from pine. Cheap benches like cheap behavior can lead to a downfall.

Folly: a foolish act or idea

A folly, as expressed in a garden scene, is usually an architectural point of interest that has no point other than to amuse. A strategically placed garden bench can be an arresting view as well as a resting place. Choose outdoor seating for style and comfort. Have you ever tried to get situated on an elaborate woven wire bench that has no cushions?

Wooden seating may be stained or even painted to blend with fences, house trim, or containers. When adding fences to your property match the tops of them to the backs of your benches, and for shear simplicity, choose benches whose backs are a lattice pattern, the easiest of all to replicate.

Attention to details can produce magic. The lack of attention can yield horrors. Remember the saying, "Everything happens for a reason." Well, that reason is usually because someone wasn't paying attention! I don't sit on white plastic chairs in my living room, and I don't intend to sit on them in the garden either. And don't get me started on "yard art"! Do you wear sweatpants to church? Please don't answer this question…

80

One of my clients said she had hired me because I said in passing, "I don't do dinky." Not only should your pathways be ample and accommodating, but your garden benches should be comfortable and properly sized. Read the definition of "folly" again. So many ornamental garden chairs and benches are like doll furniture with short legs and shallow seats. Take them directly to the fire pit! On the flip side, large logs, which would normally end up in the fire pit, can be cut into chair-height lengths, set upright, and used as seating in a woodland setting.

Make your garden a comfortable habitat for you and your friends by employing garden seating in sunny as well as shady areas for the comfort levels of various seasons and times of day.

Should you desire privacy, why not make a space strictly for one with a small table and a single cushioned chair. Additional seating can attract unwanted company while you are trying to relax and wake up with the morning paper and a cup of coffee. Sometimes a retreat that is only a door away can restore the sanity that was lost in a house full of children!

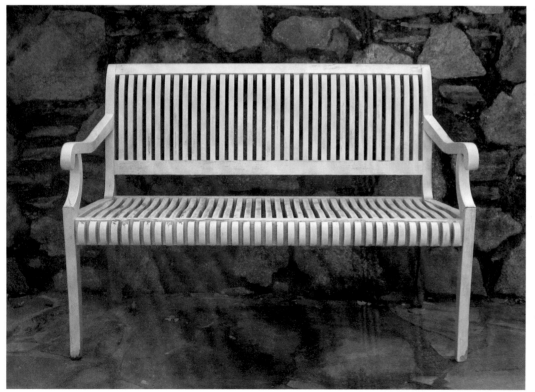

My most memorable experience with garden seating and the art of folly was, once again, at my grandmother's house in Crystal Springs, Mississippi. She and my grandfather had a giant swing set made down at the welding shop which was much taller than traditional swing sets and were fitted out with box seats that had arms and backs. Oh, the heights we could reach on that swing set!

At that point in my young life, Memama had already taught me to master the bicycle, so painting was, of course, the logical next step in my maturation process. All things seemed to happen around Easter, and this was no exception. Before Sunday school that day we had our annual pictures taken in front of the iris bed, and after Sunday school we were brought back to the house to play while the adults attended church. Wilma, who normally watched us like a hawk, was inside preparing Easter lunch as my siblings and I were preparing to get the worst spankings of our lives.

"Let's paint the swing set!" I announced, and off to the garage we went in search of supplies. We went through several cans before we found the one that suited us. The can said 'Dusty Rose', and we smeared some on the side of the garage to get a look at it. "Perfect!" we chimed.

After applying the first coat of paint to the box seats I remembered the textured ceiling in our playroom. Oh, yes…that's just the way I wanted it to look. After rummaging through the garage cabinets, I found just what I needed – granular fertilizer. We mixed the fertilizer into the paint and applied the concoction to the swing seat. They were just as I envisioned and just like our playroom ceiling.

We simply could not wait to try out the beautiful new swing set. Surely, that paint would be dry by now – it had been at least fifteen minutes.

My brother, sister, and I were laughing and waving as our parents pulled into the driveway. The laughing didn't last long, though.

The next thing we knew, Memama had us all in one bathtub and was yelling and scrubbing at the same time. I can still recall the pungent smell of the kerosene she used on us. And, there on the floor were our ruined Easter outfits – dappled in 'Dusty Rose.'

OPPOSITE: INTERIOR DESIGN BY KEITH LANGHAM.

Phillip's Tips

When selecting poolside furniture, think of comfort. For example, if no shade exists, consider a freestanding umbrella or an umbrella table.

Cushions and pillows, should be covered in fade-resistant and color-fast fabric that can be unzipped and popped into the washing machine.

Low side tables, always a good idea, are handy for holding cell phones, beverages, food and skin care products.

If some of your guests are smokers (gasp!), a small-galvanized bucket filled with coarse sand can be a tidy ashtray that isn't likely to tip over.

Choose lounge chairs that have at least one set of wheels so they can be repositioned easily. Metal furniture legs can scratch deck surfaces when dragged instead of rolled.

Thinking of furniture with vinyl straps instead of cushions? Don't. After a few minutes of sitting, your backside will look like a scored ham, and, by the way, that's suntan lotion, not glaze!

Water Features

The clipped walls would have seemed forbidding had they not been full of singing birds. I peeked through the privet archway into a small courtyard, pearl-like and mysterious. The sounds of a stream or fountain were evident, but I could not see the source.

Nothing is quite as soothing as the gurgle of a water feature, and like the scent of four o'clocks, water sounds are usually noticed before they are seen. A bit of mystery is always good, and the best gardens don't reveal all of their charms on the first date. Many gardens are beautiful at a glance, but a few improve upon close inspection. The simple song of trickling water can set the mood within a garden as can a crackling fire in your hearth.

OPPOSITE: PAUL MARCHESE, ARCHITECT. ARBORS AND POOL DESIGNED BY PHILLIP WATSON.

Phillip's Tips

If you don't plan to install an irrigation system, at least make sure that faucets are strategically placed throughout the garden for easy hose and sprinkler attachment.

The back door is typically where builders locate the outdoor faucet. However, that is also where the giant and unsightly coils of hose will be lurking.

Choose out-of-the-way spots to attach, use, and store your hoses so they are neither an eyesore nor a hazard.

My quiet spot in the garden is the patio off the kitchen whose large umbrella table allows me to relax comfortably even when it is raining. On dry days, though, I enjoy the sound of a small wall-mounted fountain as I read the newspaper and prepare for the day.

Wall mounted fountains can be used inside a home or on a screened porch. The soothing sound of water makes an afternoon nap that much sweeter. And it hasn't caused me to wet the bed, yet!

Water features needn't be expensive or fussy affairs. For simplicity, a large glazed urn with no drainage holes can be fitted with a recirculating pump. There is no need for a water connection since all water features, large and small, can be filled and replenished with a hose.

When I moved from New York City to Fredericksburg, Virginia, I desperately wanted a swimming pool but couldn't afford one. I'd have to sell a few more crops of poinsettias, first. Instead, I utilized a large clawfoot bathtub which I set up in the middle of the field, and on sunny days, I filled it halfway up with a hose and positioned myself inside. I actually felt as if I were on a pool raft, and my tan was fantastic due to the reflective qualities of the white porcelain. Of course, my neighbors thought I was crazy. They also thought I was naked. Not!

The third year I was in Fredericksburg, I finally designed and built a swimming pool. The pool was a perfect 22-foot x 22-foot square with a charcoal-colored bottom, and large slabs of grey slate which comprised the pool deck. After the pool was built, I no longer had to take summer guests on tour after tour of the historic district. Thank heavens! When supplied with music and libations my guests were content, and I was off the hook.

Dark-bottomed pools are to a garden what mirrors are to a small room. Their reflective qualities visually double the size of the space. My Virginia swimming pool, which was unheated for economic reasons, was never covered in the winter. Invariably, the center of a pool cover becomes a small pond which collects leaves, and that's a mighty big mess to look at all winter. Without the cover, the beautiful winter skies are reflected.

A dark-bottomed pool is much like a pond. If a small bit of leaf debris is on the bottom, your eyes will see the reflective surface, first, while white or blue-bottomed pools always show debris when it is present. They also look unnatural – a little too 1950s for my taste. Of course, if you like the look of roadside hotels…

CLOCKWISE FROM TOP RIGHT: Tall and slender Juniperus communis 'Pencil Point;' Equisetum hymele; fountain at the Atlanta Botanical Gardens designed by Christine Sibley; and a stream bordered by Acorus 'Variegata.'

92

I leave my pool lights on every night and all year. It's the ultimate garden lighting and a pleasure to see from the house. My pool lights are situated on the submerged wall of the pool nearest the house. The idea is to see the effect of the light, not its source.

After moving from Virginia to Atlanta, I built a similar dark-bottomed pool as well as an additional water feature. When I was on Fire Island in the early 1970s I came to really enjoy the outdoor shower at the hotel which was private, but open to the sky. Finally, I have one of my own, and it is magnificent. Ground level beds full of water-loving plants like horsetail, calla lilies, and sweet flag surround the shower area whose outdoor speakers allow me to enjoy music as I bathe. It has also turned into the best place to bathe my dog. If he gets away from me, at least he isn't running all over the house.

Once the shower was completed, the contractor asked me how I liked it. I responded, "Mission accomplished – I do feel like the baby Moses in the bulrushes!"

The same sorts of plants used around the outdoor shower are appropriate for wetland and bog gardens. If you enjoy habitat gardening, these are the gardens for you.

The first time I heard them, they sounded like a bunch of baby chickens. I suppose that is why they are called "peepers." These small frogs herald the arrival of spring even before the forsythia blooms. Peeper frogs are small and can camouflage themselves to blend with tree bark, lichens, moss and stone, and that first spring in Virginia my wetland garden was teeming with them. I had built the bog to accommodate my water loving pond cypress, Japanese iris, and cattails. The peepers serenaded me each night until their mating season ended which coincided with the arrival of the bullfrogs. For a short period, the frogs sang together – an evening symphony of bass and treble notes.

By early summer, I was rewarded once more by the appearance of a pair of red-winged blackbirds who promptly made a nest in last winter's cattail debris. For a while, I forgot about my parterres and clippers. Nature seemed to be doing a fine job on her own.

BELOW: Roped boxwood surrounds central fountain at The Freer Gallery in Washington, D.C. ACROSS THE BOTTOM, LEFT TO RIGHT: Backdrop of sheared Chamaecyparis 'Crippsii' with roped boxwood.

Birdhouses

B̶efore putting up birdhouses, you might consider placing a small Statue of Liberty somewhere nearby:

"Give me your tired, your poor… I lift my lamp beside the golden door."

Of course, Miss Liberty won't be necessary if you aren't one of those who has fits when sparrows move into the birdhouses. I try to love all of the birds, and the sparrows, who generally behave themselves, have the sweetest songs. Understanding nature is key to understanding life itself. I also try not to monitor who is moving into my neighborhood and simply hope they won't act up like the blue jays!

Phillip's Tips

Clean and refurbish birdhouses after Thanksgiving and before Valentine's Day. Remove all old nesting material and scrub the interiors with a long-handled sink brush, using a 2% dilution of bleach in soapy water which will kill any bird mite eggs.

OPPOSITE: Clematis 'Henrii', which is *not* short for Henrietta!

Birdhouses are effective as focal points within a garden and may be placed at the curve in a path or at the end of a long view. When placed atop posts or fences, vines can be used to complete the picture. Wrap the post or clad the fence in chicken wire because clematis, annual vines, and climbing roses appreciate the support and quickly hide the chicken wire from view.

Sometimes birdhouses are a little too cute for my taste such as the bathroom humor of a birdhouse shaped like a cat's head whose open mouth is the entrance! You may skip the next suggestion if you have a collection of garden gnomes. Choose birdhouses that coordinate with your house, garden structures, outdoor furniture, or fences. Many of the wooden birdhouses may be painted or stained to match existing garden colors.

And lastly, sometimes bird structures are a little too functional. I don't consider squirrel-proof bird feeders to be acceptable focal points. They look like the collaborative efforts of NASA and Dr. Frankenstein!

Climbers & Vines

Vines and climbers reign supreme when it comes to vertical gardening. Of course, weeping plants do the same thing, just in the other direction. Cascading vines, like honeysuckle may be planted at the tops of walls to spill over for dramatic effect. Whether cascading or climbing, vines are useful for hiding ugly walls or fences such as air-conditioning unit enclosures or trash bin corrals.

To make the most of a small garden or a tight space consider the layout of Manhattan. When space is limited, forget about sprawl and send your garden skyward by utilizing walls, fences, posts and arbors. In Nantucket, the rooftops themselves are covered in climbing roses.

Phillip's Tips

Wisteria may be pruned heavily from late spring until late August. Never prune wisteria after Labor Day. Wisteria vines set bud on old wood like the old-fashioned hydrangeas, and any pruning too late in the season will result in the removal of next year's flowers.

Climbers and vines are certainly attractive on birdhouse posts and feeders, but keep them clipped about a foot below the bottom of any bird structures.

When selecting vines for the mailbox post, choose plants without thorns or flowers that attract bees. It would be a shame if your mail carrier were stuck or stung, and your tax refund check dropped into the culvert!

Many climbing plants don't require training or a trellis, because they attach themselves to surfaces with small roots. The exquisite climbing hydrangea is such a plant. In addition to its late spring display of fragrant white blossoms, the climbing hydrangea sports beautiful glossy green foliage. Another vine that clamors without guidance is the durable Boston ivy, which turns a deep crimson in autumn and produces Concord-blue berries favored by mockingbirds. Virginia creeper, another deciduous vine with great fall color, is ideal for areas that need to be covered quickly, but remember, all things that are fast and furious are also higher maintenance.

BELOW, LEFT TO RIGHT: Wisteria covered porch in Nantucket and Japanese climbing fern. OPPOSITE: Wisteria 'Amethyst Falls.'

Slower and more deliberate climbers include clematis, climbing roses, and cross vine, which is a North American native. Cross vine, one my favorite plants, is a vine that doesn't require a trellis and can easily scale wooden barn walls and stone fences without support. Covered in deep tangerine trumpet flowers in early summer, the cross vine is a magnet for hummingbirds. I have used this delightful climber from Manhattan to Mississippi, where it is semi-evergreen. Cross vine is also drought tolerant and will yield years of beauty even if neglected.

Perhaps the most versatile of the climbers is the galloping wisteria. Once established, this plant is off to the races and can cover large pergolas and expansive fences in as little as two years. One of the more well-behaved varieties is Amethyst Falls which blooms a couple of weeks after the old fashioned Japanese varieties. This native wisteria doesn't have the old fashioned fragrance, but its blooms, which are arranged in grape-like clusters, are more beautiful. Amethyst Falls tops out at about twelve feet as opposed to the forty plus feet for Japanese wisteria and is perfect for the smaller garden or the lazy gardener. This wisteria may be trained up a post and topped at seven or eight feet to create a wisteria "tree" which is something to behold when it is positioned in the middle of the lawn.

OPPOSITE: Bignonia 'Tangerine Beauty' or cross vine.

Annual vines such as climbing black-eyed susan (Thunbergia alata), moonflowers, morning glories, and mandevilla are quick fixes for vertical surfaces. They are especially nice for those of us who desire clean arbors and trellises during the winter months.

After first frost remove all annual vines from trellises and arbors and repaint or repair them if necessary. Permanent vines such as wisteria should be lightly cleared of twig and leaf debris at this time, their final pruning having been done in late summer. Also, check vines that are attached to your house making certain they haven't gotten under shingles, inside window sills, or behind shutters. Vines are beautiful, but sometimes they don't behave beautifully.

ABOVE, LEFT TO RIGHT: Common morning glory, Mandevilla 'Crimson Red' and Thunbergia alata.

LEFT TO RIGHT: Clematis 'Multi Blue', Lonicera 'Cedar Lane' (red) and 'Sulphurea' (yellow) and Clematis viticella.

Containers & Window Boxes

My father might as well have brought home a dinosaur. I was so excited! In the back of his pickup truck were three lengths of petrified wood including the hollowed-out stump. Our farm bordered the Mississippi Petrified Forest, and Daddy had found the logs protruding from a creek bank. "Oh Daddy, can I have those for my garden?" I pleaded. They were so heavy – more like stone, which is what they were. Those petrified logs would ensure that my garden would be unlike any other.

I planted the hollowed-out parts with sedum and laid them out as they might have fallen, millions of years ago. What a centerpiece! Those logs were my first plant containers, and I have been container gardening ever since.

Phillip's Tips

The number one mistake that container gardeners make: choosing pots that are too small. Plantings that require more than every-other-day watering fall into the "folly" category. Small containers are only suitable for water-thrifty plants such as sedums, succulents, and cacti.

Container gardening is something anyone can do and everyone should do. Just think – no weeding! If you have back problems, elevate the pots so no bending is required when picking or tending the flowers.

Window boxes are the easiest of all containers to maintain. Simply open the window to plant and water the boxes, but if you plan to do these tasks from the top of a ladder, upgrade your insurance first, because you are basically working without a net. A light mulching will keep the boxes from drying too rapidly and will prevent mud-splash on windows. If the bottoms of the window boxes are lined with filter cloth, dirt stains won't appear on the walls below the boxes. Finally, place a two-inch layer of styrofoam peanuts directly on the filter cloth before filling the boxes. Keeping window boxes as light as possible prevents bowing and buckling.

The mobility of container plantings makes them the great variable in a garden since they may be rearranged at a whim and hand-trucked to another area. Also, should you live the life of a gypsy, window boxes, pots, and other container plantings can be taken with you at anytime of the year without any shock to the plants because no digging is involved. If your pots are petrified wood, however, hire a mover!

TOP RIGHT: Sweet potatoes produced by 'Margarita' and 'Blackie'. OPPOSITE: The chartreuse foliage of the sweet potato, 'Margarita.'

LEFT: Rainbow chard and pansies. Both are edible.
CENTER: Red verbena with red gerber daisies. RIGHT:
Salvia 'Victoria Blue' with dwarf zinnias.

Lightweight pots are popular because they are easy to move. However, use heavy weight marble chips for drainage if the plants are or will become tall. The marble ballast will prevent the pots from blowing over during storms. Another tip: if pots dry out too rapidly, consider a deep saucer as a reservoir. A light mulch prevents surface drying. Spanish moss, by the way, is a very attractive mulch when allowed to drape over the sides of the container.

One needn't spend huge amounts of money on containers. After all, it's about the plants – right? If your planters aren't particularly attractive, use cascading plants at the edges to hide the arrangement's humble foundation.

When growing up in rural Mississippi, I was amazed by the porch gardens on the other side of town. Planters fashioned from old enamel cookware, discarded sinks and tubs, and spent tires lined porches, driveways, and paths. Wandering jew spilled over the sides of some of them while others held a variety of annuals including zinnias, marigolds, and petunias. The containers were barely noticeable because the plantings were so nice. They had been cared for with love, and they were beautiful.

Moles, voles, and chipmunks can create terrific problems in the garden. To protect vulnerable plants such as hostas, lilies, and tulips, arrange them in large pots and augment the plantings with annuals and seasonal bulbs. Not only will your prized plants be spared from gnawing teeth, they will be given an elevated place of honor in the garden.

TOP RIGHT: Crown of Thorns (euphorbia). OPPOSITE: Purple shamrock (oxalis).

Everyone has space for a container garden. From windowsills to patios to balconies, potted plants provide beauty and detail.

While in Manhattan, I especially enjoyed my fire escape planters, although the fire marshal might have objected! I had a large tub of scarlet runner beans which climbed the fire escape stairs to the next floor and a singe rose bush, 'Angel Face', provided fragrance within our apartment when the windows were left open. I can still smell that rosy clove scent when I think back to those days. Although, my sowing of wild oats was at its peak in Manhattan, real gardening and old-fashioned ideas never really left me. That bit of bedrock would be my future, since the wild oats weren't about to become a cash crop!

Now, back to that fire escape. While on a luxurious (Ha!) trip to upstate New York via Greyhound bus, I visited a farm and decided to get a banty rooster. I guess I was a little homesick for Mississippi. Once back in Manhattan, I got a cage and put the rooster out on the fire escape with the scarlet runner beans. Well, as banty roosters do, "Chanticleer" crowed 24/7, and complaints from neighbors overwhelmed me, so dear Chanticleer had to go. In his place, a large pot of chicken gizzard coleus would have to suffice!

ABOVE: Angel Trumpets (datura).

Phillip's Tips

Angel trumpet blossoms are especially fragrant at night and easily measure up to ten inches in length. Expect hummingbirds and (yes, they do exist) hummingbird moths! Plant in a large pot so they may be brought inside before a hard freeze.

LEFT: Salvia 'Victoria Blue' with Nierembergia 'Lilac'.
CENTER: Mark Hampton's geranium cart. RIGHT:
Shade pots with coleus, ivy and impatiens. OPPOSITE:
'Margarita' sweet potato with red cordyline.

When winter frosts arrived, my fire escape garden looked pitiful. Big empty pots, a vacant rooster cage, and several months of winter were looking me square in the face. After my second cup of coffee, it hit me: why not put some winter-hardy plants in my containers. A spiral-cut Alberta spruce surrounded by lacey pink kale looked stunning through the living room window and satisfied my desire to have at least one clipped and controlled plant. Although the kale wouldn't last all winter, it would at least get me through football season.

Winter is too long to be without a garden. In America's southern regions, container plantings of pansies and ivy provide a colorful touch on gray winter days, but before adding those items to the planter, place daffodil, tulip, and hyacinth bulbs in the bottom. When spring arrives, you will be so proud of yourself.

In America's northern zones, you may also add bulbs to the bottoms of your pots. Plan to use some of the many dwarf conifers, which come in an array of foliage colors as permanent plantings. These "tapestry pots" are beautiful year-round, and they make fantastic house-warming gifts.

BOTTOM RIGHT: Agapanthus, Blue Lily of the Nile. OPPOSITE: My front steps lined with pots of pansies.

122

If you admire clipped plants, but don't have room for a parterre, why not try a topiary. Like the spiral-out Alberta spruce I had in New York, pre-shaped plants in a variety of forms are available at area nurseries, and only light trimming is required to maintain these topiaries.

Some people collect garden gnomes; I collect topiaries. Unfortunately, I also treat them like pets. If a pot of petunias dies while I'm on vacation, it's no big deal. But, if a topiary dies, I feel the need to mourn and, maybe, have a funeral. Owning a topiary is like owing a parrot. If properly maintained, a topiary can outlive its owner. And, I own an entire flock of them, including boxwoods, hollies, and azaleas – all trimmed and trained into fanciful shapes. Often, I've criticized friends who allowed their pet menageries to run their lives, but I really have to laugh at myself, because a menagerie of topiaries is no different.

Phillip's Tips

If the containers are beautiful, allow them to show. If not, use cascading plants to hide them.

124

Garden Paths

We all know the story about the road not taken. This is the story about the path not taken.

If pathways are rutted and collect water or are choked with weeds, no one except your dogs will use them.

Pathways should be visually inviting which can be achieved by using interesting surface materials or paving patterns. Clever path side plantings can be augmented with the occasional seating area, garden sculpture, or water feature.

Trail blazing is a grand adventure and a noble cause but somehow doesn't quite work for a garden tour. Pinched pathways and widely spaced pavers create unnecessary obstacles and challenges. Getting through life is hard enough; being led down the garden path should be a cinch!

Phillip's Tips

Remember "The Princess and the Pea"? Don't use pea gravel for pathways: it gets in your shoes.

Another tip: Keep a small stockpile of the surface material to freshen the pathways each spring.

So often pathways are created as if they were never meant to be used. Three and a half feet is the standard minimum width. However, a four foot path allows plants to spill over and soften the edges without tripping travelers.

Bordering pathways with beautiful plantings or even container plantings makes the journey interesting, and for architectural detail, paths may be lined with low, clipped hedges of boxwood or holly. Pushing those hedges a couple of feet from the path's edge allows space for interior flower borders which may be filled with colorful annuals, seasonal bulbs, or just ground covers.

If you plan to use stepping-stones or spaced pavers, low plants such as thyme and golden lysimachia may be grown between them. When laying out stones or large pavers, keep them close

ABOVE: 'Red Riding Hood' dwarf tulips with blue grape hyacinths, bordered by 'Green Velvet' boxwood. ABOVE CENTER AND OPPOSITE: Golden creeping jenny, lysimachia.

enough together so that one may walk the path without playing hopscotch. The journey down the path should be pleasant and easy to navigate without having to be overly careful of ones step.

For a percolating path (No, coffee is not involved!) use loose materials such as crushed limestone, oyster shell, or lava rock contained within an edging. "Perk" means that it drains well.

When building a loose path, create a four inches deep bed of coarse sand before applying three to four inches of surface material, which means the trench needs to be seven to eight inches deep. The loose materials allow your pathways to function as French drains and should remain free of puddles and ice at all times.

If occasional weeds appear in the pathways, carefully apply an herbicide spray because pulling weeds up through the loose material also pulls up soil from below, which will dirty the path. For persistent weeds, like oxalis, which arrive by seed apply a pre-emergent every month from last frost until first frost to prevent germination.

Hard surfaced paths needn't be plain concrete. Alternate materials include brick, which may be laid in a variety of patterns, regular and rough-cut stone, and frost proof tile.

For those who hate to weed, hard impervious (non-perking) surfaces work best. A simple push of the broom will generally keep them clean. In shady or damp areas, occasional power washing prevents the buildup of moss and algae, which can make surfaces slippery.

We also know the old saying that life is about the journey and not about the destination. A garden path's destination could be an elaborate gazebo or a screened pavilion. Or, perhaps an open field with a central fire pit. However, some paths are great circles that take one through woodland areas or parallel flower borders. Whether a path has an ending point or is circuitous, the journey itself should be worth the effort, because there are no guarantees that destinations will be reached.

And one more thing, saving for a rainy day and saving just to be saving aren't the same thing. At some point, you need to cash in your chips to receive your reward. Sometimes the rainbow is so beautiful that one can forget about the pot of gold. It's the journey, and the path that was taken.

Foliage

As my friend Rosemary Verey pointed out to me, good foliage can carry the day when the flowers aren't blooming, and after visiting many of the famous gardens in England, it became clear that she was right.

In America, brightly colored foliage is seen more often in commercial settings than in private gardens.

Is strictly green foliage a sign of modesty or a lack of nerve? Well, the bottom line is the same: it's dull! And according to Rosemary, "It's a sin to be dull."

Phillip's Tips

Beautiful foliage allows a garden to shine without flowers. Handsome leaves are also a welcome addition to flower arrangements.

Utilize variegated, golden, silver and burgundy foliage to spice up your garden.

In England, interesting foliage abounds. Many of the annuals and perennials sport fancy and colorful leaves, which make them attractive even when they aren't in bloom. The larger members of the landscape, the trees and shrubs, often have silver, burgundy, gold, or variegated foliage. Green foliage is certainly nice, but within the shadows can almost disappear. Adding a group of 'Patriot' hostas to the center of a shade garden is like turning on a spotlight. The pure white edges of 'Patriot' illuminate even the darkest recesses of the garden. Want a bit more color? Try the glorious ground cover, Lysimachia nummularia 'Aurea' for a golden Midas touch along woodland paths. Conversely, to create shadow in sunny areas, include dark-foliaged plants such as Berberis 'Crimson Pigmy'. When paired with silver Artemisias like 'Powis Castle' or Dusty Miller, the dark

ABOVE, LEFT TO RIGHT: Cordyline 'Red Sensation', Yucca 'Gold Sword', and coleus and yucca. OPPOSITE: Dusty Miller.

berberis pops even more. Even when used alone, the cool silvers and grays of the Artemisias are a welcome relief during the dog days of summer.

Another of my favorite plant pairings is the sweet potato 'Margarita' (bright chartreuse) teamed with her sister 'Blackie' (purplish black). The vines weave in and out of one another, creating an arresting arrangement of beautiful foliage. These two sweet potatoes are also happy as clams in a container and will spill over the sides creating a colorful waterfall. In addition to their beauty, these annual vines cover large areas quickly, thus stretching the garden budget.

For a similar contrast, try permanent plantings of Japanese maples. Countless varieties exist, and many have highly contrasting foliage such as bright yellow and deep burgundy.

Good foliage isn't just about color, however. Textures of foliage and shapes of leaves provide uniqueness to the garden. Consider the spiky elegance or 'Gold Sword' yucca or the tropical 'Red Sensation' cordyline. These unusual plants are perfect as stand-alone specimens in containers or as a relief to the usual softness of a flower border.

Ornamental grasses, which come in a variety of sizes and colors, are also nice punctuation points. Many, like the exceptional dwarf pampas, produce plumes in late summer, which can be dried

BELOW: Dwarf pampas grass plumes. RIGHT: Copper fennel in bloom.

and added to arrangements for height. The dwarf pampas is evergreen in the Deep South.

Another grass, the graceful miscanthus, practically dances in summer breezes and adds movement and magic to flower borders. 'Caberet' is the finest of the miscanthus group and has deep margins of white variegation.

If a garden is overly reliant on flowers, there will be periods of time when it is in a funk. Beautiful leaves can bridge those flowerless gaps and provide an even flow of year-round interest. Use some of that great foliage in arrangements, and pick fewer flowers to avoid denuding the garden.

A vase full of miscanthus foliage or pampas plumes is elegant and can provide the height that most flower arrangements can't achieve. Be bold and inventive. Like my great aunt, Eloise, who invented the dried catalpa leaf arrangement, I am also a fan of occasional reckless abandon!

Colorful evergreen foliage, which needn't be green, brightens winter days and lifts spirits. In bleak December when all of those flowers that were so beautiful in the summer are absent, use blue

ABOVE RIGHT: Petunias are paired with colorful croton foliage. BOTTOM RIGHT: Salvia argentea. BELOW: 'Autumn' fern with purple Persian Shield.

spruce and variegated boxwood for holiday wreaths and table and mantle decorations. "Deck the halls!"

The golden spires of Chamaecyparis 'Crippsii' that were planted as a backdrop for my swimming pool in Virginia, stand out like shafts of light twelve months of the year and require only one annual trimming. Although it took a decade to get them to perfection, they were easily the lowest maintenance and the highest interest of any of my clipped plants. Leyland cypress, on the other hand, proved to be extremely high maintenance with up to four trimmings per year. The leylands were fast and furious but also weak and short-lived.

If intelligent plant choices are made for the long-term, your garden won't be falling apart when you are. Old age should have SOME comforts! Who knows – like the reblooming German iris, you may get a second wind in the autumn of your life.

BELOW: Variegated aucuba. TOP RIGHT: Annual coleus. BELOW RIGHT: Weeping Japanese maples. OPPOSITE: Iris germanica 'Batik.'

Iris & Lilies

Every time I smell bearded German iris I'm back at my grandmother's house, all dressed up in my new Easter suit. Before I learned what the irises were, I thought their exposed roots were potatoes!

Nostalgia is an active part of my life and, in some ways, is the passion in my garden designs. Heirloom and gift plants have a magical way of reminding us of "past perfect" times and allow departed loved ones to maintain a presence in our lives. When I smell the bearded iris, I can almost feel my grandmother hugging me.

Gardens can be intimate spaces where childhood joys are reawakened, and simple pleasures are enough. We forget how as children, we were amazed by the flight of a dragonfly, the sudden song of a catbird, or the twinkling of fireflies on an August night.

The scent of freshly cut grass still reminds me of summer vacation. And the pungent smell of burning leaves lets me know that Thanksgiving is nigh. Always a nail-biter, I recall the bitter taste of my fingers after picking a bunch of daffodils. It's all small stuff, but somehow it paints the big picture that is life.

Phillip's Tips

Siberian iris come in a wide range of colors, but the blue varieties are by far the best performers and provide a color unlike any of the other flowers of spring except, perhaps, the pansies.

142

The German iris, my favorite of all flowers, doesn't contribute much to the landscape once having bloomed. However, the rebloomers give a spectacular second show in September and make a solid case for themselves. German iris foliage just isn't that interesting, but no other iris is capable of reblooming. When all of the fall perennials are putting on their final performances, the reblooming German iris is giving a vivid and fragrant preview of spring.

Some iris foliages do hold their own even after blooming. The late spring blossoms of Siberian iris are followed by thick stands of upright foliage – a great vertical and spiky look which adds an architectural touch to the flower border. The foliage easily reaches 3-4' in height and maintains a fresh appearance until autumn.

For a succession of iris blooms, try the butter-yellow Iris pseudacorus. Like the Siberian iris, this "yellow flag" iris has exquisite upright foliage that is handsome all season and will grow in a variety of conditions but is ideally suited to wetland, bog, or pond gardens.

The next iris to bloom is the Louisiana iris, which is also happy to have wet feet. Louisiana irises are available in colors ranging from rich purple to terra cotta to white. The foliage, although similar to that of Iris pseudacorus, is somewhat floppy and unruly.

The final iris to bloom (discounting the reblooming German iris of September) is the Japanese iris. I prefer the variegated form simply because the foliage is fresh and interesting all summer. It too, can be used in wet areas and produces perfect lavender-blue blossoms in mid June.

After the irises have finished their shows, the true lilies, those which grow from bulbs and are unlike daylilies, take center stage. I clearly remember one particular late spring evening. I could smell the trumpet lilies even before I saw them as the night air was completely perfumed. It was August, but in April, I had set out scores of lily bulbs so I could have this moment. The perennial beds were already full, and I needed something that could emerge from them and stand tall without shading the other plants. True lilies (orientals, trumpets, and asiatics) are perfect for this. They multiply rapidly and bloom the first year.

For a summer of lilies, start with asiatics, which kick the season off in June and are closely followed by the exquisitely perfumed orientals. Late summer and early fall feature the equally fragrant trumpet lilies which tower over all of the other perennials and are great companions for the statuesque and late blooming perennial hibiscus.

With minimal investment (bulbs are much less expensive than potted perennials) and minimum effort (bulbs only need to be planted four to five inches deep), a summer of lilies is possible the very first year. All true lily varieties are rapid multipliers and investments will more than double by the second season.

144

TOP: Variegated Japanese Iris. BELOW: Yellow flag iris (Iris pseudocorus). OPPOSITE: Stargazer Oriental lily.

Whether lily bulbs are in beds or planters, they never fail to dazzle. Go ahead – pat yourself on the back and give the true lilies a high-five!

Daylilies, unlike true lilies, grow from tubers not bulbs, and are the easiest of all flowering perennials to cultivate. As an added bonus, when true lily bulbs are planted among daylilies, the daylily foliage will provide support for their taller companions.

My grandmother gave me my first daylily, a lovely soft yellow called 'Hyperion'. What I liked most about it was its light lemon fragrance. Memama simply took a sharp shovel and shoved it straight down into the daylily clump. She then removed one-half of the clump and pulled the mass of tubers apart with her hands, explaining that each small tuber mass would produce daylily

LEFT TO RIGHT: Daylily 'Chicago Apache' and Lilium 'Conca D'Or', an orienpet lily, which is a cross between an oriental and a trumpet lily. OPPOSITE: Iris sibericum.

flowers the very next season. Amazing! She also told me that daylilies are so tough they can be divided any time of year, even when they are in bloom.

"Daylilies are the backbone of the summer garden," my friend, David Winn informed me. He and I met when I first moved to Fredericksburg, Virginia. David took up where my grandmother left off, and soon I was not only dividing daylilies but also cross-pollinating them, harvesting the seeds, and developing new hybrids. He would also introduce me to reblooming daylilies which are capable of blooming the very same season they are divided. Memama would have been shocked!

Daylilies will put on a spectacular show in even the worst conditions so save the perfectly

LEFT AND CENTER: A pair of Asiatic lilies flank the spectacular reblooming German iris, 'Harvest of Memories', in bloom in late November in Atlanta. OPPOSITE: Daylily 'Zella Virginia.'

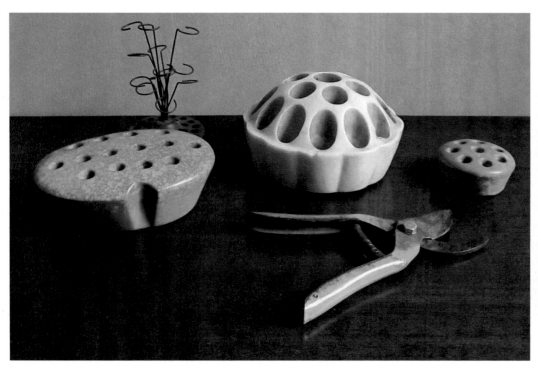

prepared beds for more finicky plants. The foolproof daylily prospers in all parts of the United States in part shade to full sun, in wet or dry conditions, and in containers or in the ground. No other perennial gives so much when it is given so little. Sounds like the ideal relationship, doesn't it?

For steep eroding banks that are impossible to mow, daylilies are the perfect solution since the plants, which have vigorous root systems, become quite dense and prevent the soil and mulch from washing away. To have continuous and carefree color on those banks from late spring to late fall, use reblooming varieties such as 'Stella d'Oro' and 'Happy Returns.'

If successful gardening has eluded you, don't despair. The faithful and reliable daylily wants to be your best friend.

Peonies

After moving from the deep South to the Mid-Atlantic region, I realized that there were more new plants for me to experience than I had ever imagined.

In Virginia, I could still have the same crape myrtles that I had had in Mississippi, but gardenias were, unfortunately, too tender. However, being able to have peonies for the first time made up for everything I couldn't have.

The peony is one of the easiest and longest-lived of all perennials and some varieties smell more like roses than roses. Single, semi-double, and large pom-pom blossoms are available in a variety of colors and all are excellent cut flowers.

If you've ever priced peony blooms at a florist shop, consider this: A bare root peony division costs about the same as one flower stem. Given that peonies, when properly planted and located, last a lifetime, what's the holdup? Homegrown blossoms that weren't shipped from overseas or kept in cold storage will last longer as cut flowers and will retain that delicious peony fragrance – not that refrigerator smell.

Phillip's Tips

Plant daffodil bulbs among the peonies for deer-proof flowers that will precede the peonies. As the peony foliage emerges, it covers the yellowing daffodil leaves quite nicely.

Peonies must have a substantial frost in order to do well. I see a few stragglers in Atlanta, but northern Georgia is about the southern limit for those beauties.

When purchasing bare root divisions, be careful to plant them correctly. Notice the small pink eyes attached to the woody crab-like tubers. These eyes should not be more than two inches beneath the soil surface and spacing should be thirty inches, allowing room for the peony clumps to develop. The gaps between the immature peonies may be filled with annuals until the peony "hedge" is realized. The more sun the peonies receive, the quicker they will mature.

Apply a light layer of shredded mulch to protect your new plants from winter soil heaving. The mulch cuts down on weed competition the first year and allows the peonies to stay evenly moist as they establish themselves.

Fertilization is important to build good root systems, strong flower stems, and unblemished foliage. Dehydrated cow manure is a good organic fertilizer that also improves the soil structure, but if commercial chemical fertilizers are preferred, slow release varieties in pelleted form work well. Especially be wary of rough granular fertilizers as they can burn the bases of new shoots.

For immediate results and quick fixes, liquid fertilizers (ready to use or mix your own) are desirable. One final word of caution: do not apply any of these fertilizers to freshly planted bare root peonies or bare root anything, instead waiting until new foliage has emerged and has hardened-off.

Even after the late spring peony blooms have finished, the deep green hedge-like foliage remains lush and attractive until the first frost of autumn.

If you live in an area that is graced by or infested with deer (opinions vary!), the peony is ideal, because the deer won't eat any part of this perennial. Plant daffodil bulbs among the peonies for deer-proof flowers that will precede the peonies. As the peony foliage emerges, it covers the yellowing daffodil leaves quite nicely. For follow-up blooms among the peonies, add basils and salvias. These tall deer-proof annuals will be nicely supported by the stiff peony foliage and will bloom freely through autumn. And there you have it, three periods of interest in the same spot. It's not quite a three-ring circus, but it's still one of the greatest shows in the garden.

Summer Bounty

When I think of summer, I remember tomato sandwiches, arrangements of zinnias and dahlias, and naps on screened porches. This most bountiful time of year is the season for pool parties, outdoor barbeques, and family reunions. Sharing the bounty of the garden with friends and neighbors can cement relationships for years. Baskets of fresh tomatoes, fruit jar arrangements of flowers, and homemade preserves can awaken memories of loved ones and happy times. The old-fashioned flavors of heirloom tomatoes can be yours as they were your grandmother's, and those zinnias that remind you of her garden club arrangements can easily be grown, even in a small garden.

Consolidation is the key when limited garden space is the issue. Add a row of zinnias to the vegetable garden, and everything from the main course to the centerpiece can be harvested in one location. For smaller garden spaces, consider container gardening.

New and heirloom varieties of vegetables and herbs are just as beautiful as any blooming plants. Dainty yellow pear tomatoes, colorful ornamental sweet potatoes, and the elegant 'Pesto Perpetuo' basil (variegated!) add zest to container plantings as well as to the dinner table. The edible landscape!

Phillip's Tips

Here's a little tomato trick my father taught me. Tomatoes are one of the few plants that can be planted several inches deeper than they are in their nursery pots. Deeply planted tomatoes send out additional roots from the buried stems which will enable them to take up larger amounts of water and nutrients. The expanded root systems provide great support for the tomato plants that will be laden with fruit later in the season. Give the tomato plants as much sun as possible to ensure a bountiful harvest.

Did you know that those fancy ornamental sweet potatoes actually make sweet potatoes? It's easy to focus on the gorgeous leaves of 'Margarita' (chartreuse) and 'Blackie' (black-purple), but something magical is happening underground.

For a dynamic duo, plant ornamental sweet potatoes at the base of heirloom tomato plants. The heirloom tomatoes will climb up the tomato cage and the sweet potatoes will cascade to the ground, forming a pool of colorful leaves. After the first frost, dump out the pot and harvest those delicious sweet potatoes whose taste is somewhere between chestnuts and yams.

Not so fond of sweet potatoes? Add variegated basil at the edge of your tomato planter which can be used in pesto or as part of an heirloom tomato salad.

Many "new" varieties of heirloom tomatoes are available these days, and each one has a unique flavor. Have you priced these babies at the grocery store? The many varieties available range from yellow to red to purple. Some are ideal for salads, some for sandwiches, and some for cooking. A favorite of mine is the deliciously robust 'Cherokee Purple'. For a salad that is tasty and visually appetizing, pair it with the small yellow pear tomato. Yellow tomatoes, by the way, are ideal for those on low-acid diets. Other worthy varieties include 'Russian 117' (sandwiches), 'Principe Bourgese' (sauces), 'Green Zebra' (salads), 'Mortgage Lifter' (stuffed), and 'Mr. Stripey' (fried).

Heirloom tomatoes hold a special place in my heart. In the early 1980s I purchased an old nursery in Fredericksburg, Virginia, called Wine's Greenhouses. Mr. and Mrs. Wine raised all manner of plants for sale but were best known for their unusual tomatoes. Many were local favorites that had been passed down from generation to generation.

Heirloom varieties are always tastier than the often pithy tomatoes found in grocery stores. Why grow the same varieties that are available in the produce section? Store-tomatoes were developed for long shelf lives and easy shipping. Thick skins that cover bland and mealy innards make for durable if tasteless tomatoes.

Nearly all heirloom tomato plants are climbers and require caging, but don't try to accomplish

CLOCKWISE FROM TOP RIGHT: Canna 'Tangelo', Chrysanthemum 'Gold Gigi', Dahlia 'Gold Crown', and Gaillardia 'Fanfare'. OPPOSITE: Gaillardia 'Red and Yellow.'

this with stakes. You will be sorry. In full sun, which is preferable, the tomato plants may attain heights in excess of six feet. They are ideally suited to large containers on decks or patios, although traditional in-ground planting works beautifully.

Nothing is finer than fresh tomatoes from your own garden. And, your neighbors will enjoy a basket of heirloom tomatoes a lot more than that sack of horrible zucchini you abandoned on their doorstep like an unwanted baby!

Enough about tomatoes.

I hope everyone is full, and that we can move along to the flowers of summer. While the vegetable garden is churning out produce like a food bank, the flower borders are brimming with color, fragrance and texture.

For shear drama, nothing is going to out-do the perennial hibiscus which comes in a wide range of colors including hot pink, lipstick red, soft lavender, and primrose yellow. All varieties are fully cold hardy in most parts of the United States, unlike their tropical hibiscus cousins.

CLOCKWISE FROM RIGHT: Rudbeckia 'Autumn Sun', Rudbeckia 'Goldsturm' and sunflowers with Rudbeckia 'Goldsturm'. OPPOSITE: Summer's bounty includes sliced heirloom tomatoes, baby radishes, fingerling carrots, string beans, sugar snaps and yellow bell peppers.

Some varieties top out at three and a half feet in height while others may exceed eight feet. Late summer bloomers, these glorious flowers can be up to twelve inches in diameter – bigger than that baby's head! Perennial hibiscus should be situated in full sun and may be under planted with other late-season bloomers like coneflowers, black-eyed susans, gaillardias, and 'Sheffield' chrysanthemums. Although the hibiscus blooms last only a day, they are beautiful when floated singly in a low bowl. The other flowers mentioned have long vase lives and, like perennial hibiscus, will come back and multiply each year in your garden.

Weaning the garden from an over abundance of annuals is a good economical move which also allows the garden to have a changing character. Early summer perennials such as Shasta daisies, coreopsis, and asiatic lilies are followed in the mid-summer by summer phlox, daylilies, and various salvias. Late summer heralds the arrival of the apricot-hued 'Sheffield' chrysanthemums, 'Autumn Joy' sedum, and the towering hollyhocks.

Annuals certainly have a purpose, however, and like beautiful foliage, they bridge the gaps that occur in perennial blooming schedules. The annuals provide a common thread that stitches the garden together from mid-spring through fall.

CLOCKWISE FROM BELOW: Blue plumbago, giant marigolds and pansies, which are beautiful throughout the summer and into autumn in areas with cool night temperatures.

If all you remember about annuals is impatiens for shade/vinca for sun, you will be all right. Don't be afraid to be adventuresome, though. Conservatively, perhaps trying a new variety of salvia or any other plant whose name you recognize can be your daring garden statement, but sometimes total strangers can become friends for life. The nice thing about plants is they don't keep calling once the honeymoon is over. Be brutal and discard what doesn't work, considering it a cheap divorce. Trials and tribulations occur, but "for better or worse" needn't apply to your garden.

New and better varieties of plants are being developed all the time, and many almost forgotten older varieties still have the magic touch. Expand your garden repertoire beyond the tried and true plants which are sometimes about as interesting as those old classmates at the high school reunion who only talk of the 'glory days' because, apparently, nothing of interest has happened since.

A few familiar or heirloom plants are fine for a nostalgic framework, but use new plant "friends" to provide the spark for an exciting and very current garden.

RIGHT: Orange California poppy. BELOW: Summer phlox by pool.

OPPOSITE: KEN TATE, ARCHITECT.

Phillip's Tips

Having fresh flowers and beautiful foliage to cut is one of life's great pleasures. Rarely do I buy flowers for my house having planted perennials, annuals, and shrubs, which provide fresh cuts most of the year. A florist's arrangement is an expense; a productive garden is an investment, which yields a constant and replenishing supply of materials for your own unique arrangements.

New varieties of plants simply thrill me. Discovering nandina with yellow berries in Raleigh, North Carolina, nearly made me crazy. I bought every one that would fit into my truck, and soon every garden I designed had a signature yellow-berried nandina! But that was just the beginning of my rare plant insanity.

"I'll hold my coat over you, just be quick," Rosemary instructed as she handed me the clippers. Mrs. Verey and I had given a lecture together that day in Raleigh, and we were now at the esteemed J.C. Raulston Arboretum. As we looked over the trial beds of new plant introductions, a wave of kleptomania overtook me. After collecting several cuttings of new and commercially unavailable plants, we headed for the exit. How stealthy we felt! Just before reaching the gate with bulging pockets, we were greeted by none other than J.C. Raulston, himself. He, of course had recognized the famous English garden doyenne. Mr. Raulston inquired whether Rosemary and I had gotten what we had come for. My face turned as red as a poinsettia as he introduced himself to me. That day I joined the arboretum as a professional, and from then on was allowed to take a few cuttings LEGALLY!

CLOCKWISE FROM RIGHT: Cascading petunias, hardy perennial hibiscus, 'Lord Baltimore' and dwarf Meyer lemon tree.

168

ABOVE RIGHT: Celosia 'Flamingo Feather.'

That was a mighty long story about rare and unusual plants, but it had to be told. If your garden is to be personal and as unique as you are, adventures are necessary. Plants collected on vacations or ordered from far away nurseries will increase the interest of the garden as well as your interest *in* the garden.

Summer is all about the garden, and the kids are out of school, which means help may be available. A roadside stand of heirloom tomatoes will bring in a lot more than a traditional lemonade stand, and it's a great way to get your children interested in gardening. Of course, many of the summer cut flowers like dahlias, zinnias, and gladiolas, can be sold alongside the heirloom tomatoes.

Last summer my garden was so beautiful that I decided to stay put instead of traveling. Each day I brought garden-cut flowers and foliage into the house just for me to enjoy. I saw my resident doves raise two sets of babies, and I officially declared war on the marauding chipmunks. I enjoyed the sunrises, sunsets, and full moons which brought different qualities of light to the garden and enabled me to see it in a "different light." Much of this writing was done that summer, and I finally felt like Atlanta was my home.

Phillip's Tips

Always use scissors or clippers when harvesting tomatoes, squash or peppers. Pulling them from the plants often damages the stems. Clean clippers in bleach before moving to the next plant.

The smell of fresh mown grass filled the air as I pushed the rotary mower across my grandfather's lawn, creating a beautiful striped effect. Each Saturday I mowed Granddaddy's yard so I'd have money for the school dance that night. I *lived* for those dances! Sometimes, I made a little extra by picking wild blackberries along the fence rows of our farm. Unlike the new blackberry hybrids, these were full of thorns. However, the berries were delicious, and I always could count on our cook, Minnie, to make the best blackberry cobbler I ever laid lips to. Some years later, my father tried his hand at blueberries. He succeeded where most Southerners fail, because he chose a variety particularly suited to the deep South, one of the rabbiteye blueberry cultivars. Oh, he was proud, and the whole family was amazed. Daddy could actually grow something besides cotton! It wasn't until I moved to Virginia at age thirty that I had strawberries. Mr. and Mrs. Wine, from whom I bought my property, had left their strawberry patch for me, and it was bountiful, but only as long as I kept it weeded. It soon became such a job that I almost gave up. A friend suggested that I put the strawberry plants in large whiskey barrels. Not only did they produce better, but no more wire grass could creep in. They were also out of reach of the rabbits. I'm telling you, fresh flowers are glorious in summer, but how about blackberry cobbler, strawberry shortcake, and blueberry pie!

ABOVE: Buddleia 'Santana' is a magnet for butterflies as are all salvias. OPPOSITE: Salvia patens 'Oceana Blue' with silver Artemisia 'Powis Castle'.

Index

Phillip's Tips

If you are not much of a gambler or are afraid of change, try to find ways to venture beyond your comfort zone. Trying a new perennial or unfamiliar shrub or tree could be just the thing you need to shine. And, because you are a cautious and clever soul, you chose a nursery that guarantees its plants for a full year! Now, wasn't that easy?

OPPOSITE: KEN TATE, ARCHITECT.

Phillip's Tips

The impossible premise of a no-maintenance garden still manages to fool some folks. I mean, even asphalt driveways need SOME maintenance! A perfectly designed garden is only as good as its maintenance. Hard surfaces that may be swept or hosed-off are lower maintenance than loose surfaces, and ground cover beds are easier to tend than flower beds. However, the lower the maintenance, the lower the interest. It's like raising a baby; if you don't intend to do it well, you'd better not have one.

177

Phillip

in 1979

Appreciation

Thank you…

When I was twelve years old my Aunt Irene who owned Watson's Flower Box taught me how to root chrysanthemum cuttings. She had a small greenhouse behind her florist shop, and one weekend she gave me my first plant propagation lesson.

"Oh, Mama, look!" I held up the freshly rooted chrysanthemum cuttings for her to admire. "See what Irene taught me – it's like magic!" I exclaimed. And it was. We had made plants out of sticks. I could scarcely wait for the new plants to grow so I could take even more cuttings

Already, the kitchen window was brimming with jelly jars and Coke bottles holding various stems that would root in water. Coleus was by far the easiest, but soon I began to use rooting hormones to propagate euonymus, boxwood, and hydrangea cuttings.

I simply loved the beautiful foliage displayed by the different coleus plants. Russell's Feed Store always had a nice assortment of them grown in small peat pots. After school, I would stop by to see if any new plants had arrived. The money I normally spent on candy at Rhine's Store now went towards expanding my coleus collection. As I took more and more cuttings from my original plants, they began to achieve a compact and groomed habit. When I look back, I realize that those coleus plants were my first topiaries.

The quickness of the coleus perfectly matched my disposition. Topiaries out of boxwood and holly, which take years to develop, would have to wait until I could become a bit more patient.

Thanks for loving me, Irene.

Sue Seratt – For always being Sue. I love you.

Cynthia Helms – Who allowed me to dismantle one of Jim van Sweden's gardens

John and Linda Coker – My keepers in Fredericksburg, Virginia, who allow me to make their home mine.

Amy Pennington – Whose generosity and kindness helped me to finish this book. Thanks for Aspen.

Mike and Carolyn Deaver – For taking me to my first Philadelphia Flower Show and for making me feel like I belonged there.

Bryant Clifford – Brilliant artist, whose companionship was a beautiful chapter in my life.

Jane and Vaughn Dunn – Thanks for trusting me to design a garden for you and for introducing me to dear Christine.

Sybil Connolly – A true lady, who took an interest in me and pretty much got me invited to exhibit at the New York Flower Show.

Elvin McDonald – Whose recommendations led to my career on TV. You changed my life and I am forever grateful.

Allen Burrows – Brilliant plantsman and the most interesting person I know. And a real smarty-pants!

Jim Barksdale – A man of quiet strength and boundless curiosity who simply enjoys all sorts of people.

Tom Woodham – A friend after all these years who gave me my first job after college and who still remembers my "unusual and illustrated" resume.

Sharon Lieber Holland – Dear "Squash Basket"

Will Edgar – Who taught me that good designs should command good fees. Decent and talented and honest.

Suzanne and Ramsey Frank – For accepting me as an equal and for allowing me to design exactly what I envisioned for their property. And for the Aston Martin!

Ryan Gainey – Whose love of rare plants and rare people made me pay attention.

Jamie Moore – Junior high school teacher who believed I was a good writer and whose friendship I continue to cherish.

Jim Ashmore – My trusty garden man, for making life more interesting – aliens and all!

David Nickels – We've outlasted everyone else. Now what? Party on!

Daddy – Thanks for the petrified wood, the fantail pigeons, and the deer camp.

Mother – Beautiful and brilliant, for encouraging me to study horticulture and for her bed of 'Tropicana' roses.

David Winn – My first gardening guru.

Gary Cobb – Whose beautiful plants make my job of presenting them a pleasurable endeavor.

Catherine Strange – Whose early guidance and continuing support have made this book dream a reality.

Carolyn Davis – Whose discerning eye allows her to literally paint with plants. A+

Stephen Wesley – For his steadfast friendship and the Kentucky Derby.

John Evans and Lemuria.

Roslyn Mann – Who made it possible for me to own the right vehicle when I first began my career in New York.

Bonny Martin – Thanks for introducing me to Ronaldo Maia and for booking my very first garden lecture in Memphis.

Scott Blake – My right-hand man for so many years who taught me much of what I know about plants.

Jim Freid – It's been quite a journey, Jim, and I thank you for taking a chance on me and allowing me to bring the "sizzle."

Mark Higdon – Whose friendship and design talents bring a lot to my life.

Cathie Newell – My long-suffering office manager and friend, who tolerates my mood swings and unreasonable expectations.

Nina Campbell – For dancing with me all night in Annapolis and for cooking dinner for me in London.

Bryan Ramsey – Whose drafting skills and design refinements make my projects shine brighter.

Ken Tate – Brilliant architect who always credits my work and whose creations provide nice homes for my gardens.

Charles Cresson – For introducing me to the Lavendula Society and for taking me to Taylor's Nursery in Raleigh, North Carolina.

Wayne Gootee – My #1 critic, who monitors my physique and shames me into shape!

John and Patricia Chadwick – Whose friendship is unwavering.

Keith Langham – For tricking Alease into hiring me.

Virginia Griffee – My only sister and my biggest fan. Honesty and integrity do provide rewards.

Tony Fulton – Expert groundsman, who makes my projects shine and whose instincts and suggestions are stellar.

Panteleon, dear Leon – Who is as good as gold and is the most decent human being I have ever met. Your gardening skills are unequalled.

Howard Kurtzman – Who told me I was on the wrong path…and I believed him. Thank you, thank you.

Alease Fisher – Dearest friend and provocateur, who lovingly points out the blind spots in my brilliant field of vision!

Dan Overly – Who taught me how to develop a habitat garden and whose gentle and generous nature show others that kindness does make a difference.

Jerry Harpur – For photographing me and my gardens and for making all look more attractive than they actually were.

My dog, Dutch – Who has seen 'em come around the bend and then go over the hill. As he looks out the window at the disappearing tail-lights, I half expect him to say, "And I'm still here."

My friend, John Holland, who recently was rocking out for thirty minutes to a Janis Joplin video, only to discover at the end that it was actually Led Zeppelin, has been a great friend to me for many many years. Most of those friends from our early days in New York are long gone. They burned fast and bright and then went out. Just like Janis. A roll of the dice? Dumb luck? I have no idea, but I am thankful for every day on this Earth. Some of those shooting stars were quite dazzling and left a trail of fascinating memories. Thank God you are still here, John.

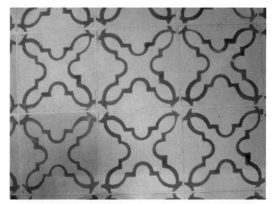

Notes

Phillip's Tips

A garden journal is ideal for keeping plant names as well as their locations in the garden. Labels are often lost, so a record is invaluable, particularly if you'd like to acquire more of a certain plant. If the nursery guarantees its plants, tuck the receipts into your journal, too.

Notes

Phillip's Tips

Small pots of chives, oregano, or parsley make ideal gifts and can easily be grown in sunny windows. These plants will be around longer than an arrangement of flowers and especially longer than a bottle of wine. Cheers!

187

Notes

_____

_____

_____

_____

_____

_____

_____

_____

_____

_____

_____

_____

_____

_____

_____

_____

_____

_____

_____

_____

_____

_____

Phillip's Tips

Plant winter blooming shrubs and perennials to help off-set the doldrums of cold and bleak days. Camellias, winter jasmine, witch hazel, and hellebores are excellent candidates. Why wait for the crocus and the early daffodils? Seize the season!

Notes

_____
_____
_____
_____
_____
_____
_____
_____
_____
_____
_____
_____
_____
_____
_____
_____
_____
_____
_____
_____

Phillip's Tips

Plant a cutting garden. It's simple, it's convenient, and it makes good economic sense. Lily, hardy gladiola, and daffodil bulbs are inexpensive, easy to plant, and come back year after year. Other great perennials for cutting include liatris, crocosmia, and gaillardia. Wean yourself from the florist and vow to only nurse your garden!